BROADMAN COMMENTS APR.-MAY '97

8 Ready-To-Teach Bible Study Lessons

8 Ready-To-Teach Bible Study Lessons

ROBERT J. DEAN
J. B. FOWLER, JR.
JAMES E. TAULMAN

Based on the International Sunday School Lessons
Each Plan Includes These Sections : ❀ Studying the Bible
❀ Applying the Bible ❀ Teaching the Bible

BROADMAN
& HOLMAN
PUBLISHERS

Nashville, Tennessee

This material was first published in *Broadman Comments, 1996–1997*

4217-46
ISBN: 0-8054-1746-X

The Outlines of the International Sunday School Lessons, Uniform Series, are copyrighted by the Committee on the Uniform Series and are used by permission.

Dewey Decimal Classification: 268.61
Printed in the United States of America

Broadman Comments *is published quarterly by Broadman & Holman Publishers, 127 Ninth Avenue, North, Nashville, Tennessee 37234*

When ordered with other church literature, it sells for $4.99 per quarter. Second class postage paid at Nashville, Tennessee

ISSN: 0068-2721

POSTMASTER: Send address change to *Broadman Comments,* Customer Service Center, 127 Ninth Avenue, North Nashville, Tennessee 37234

WRITERS

STUDYING THE BIBLE

Robert J. Dean continues the theological traditions of *Broadman Comments* while adding his own fresh insights. Dean is retired from the Baptist Sunday School Board, and is a Th.D. graduate of New Orleans Seminary

APPLYING THE LESSON

J. B. Fowler, Jr. is a freelance writer from San Antonio, Texas. He was formerly editor of *Baptist New Mexican* of the New Mexico Baptist Convention.

TEACHING THE CLASS

James E. Taulman is a freelance writer in Nashville, Tennessee. Prior to that, Taulman was an editor of adult Sunday school materials for the Baptist Sunday School Board.

ABBREVIATIONS AND TRANSLATIONS

Scripture passages are from the authorized King James Version of the Bible. Other translations used:

Contents

HOPE FOR THE FUTURE
Studies in Revelation

April

LETTERS TO CHURCHES

Apr. 6 — Commanded to Write........................ 2
Apr. 13 — To Smyrna and Pergamum 10
Apr. 20 — To Thyatira 17
Apr. 27 — To Philadelphia and Laodicea 24

May

A MESSAGE OF HOPE

May 4 — The Redeeming Lamb 31
May 11— Provision for the Redeemed.................... 39
May 18— The Victorious Christ....................... 46
May 25— A New Heaven and Earth 53

Hope for the Future
Studies in Revelation*

INTRODUCTION

April's lessons, entitled "Letters to Churches," have an introductory lesson on Revelation 1, which contains Jesus' command for John to write to the seven churches of Asia. Then there are three lessons from Revelation 2–3, dealing with the Lord's messages to five of the seven churches.

"A Message of Hope" is the theme of May's studies and centers on reasons for hope and encouragement for God's people presented in selected passages in Revelation. One lesson presents the Lamb of God as worthy of all praise. Another lesson pictures the redeemed people of God worshiping the Lamb who has delivered them through great sufferings. A third lesson depicts the victory over evil by Christ and the judgment based on the book of life. The final lesson points to the glories of the new heaven and new earth.

---

*These studies include only two months of lessons due to the conversion of the Sunday school curriculum for 1997 to seasonal quarters.

Commanded to Write

Basic Passage: Revelation 1:1–20
Focal Passage: Revelation 1:4–15

The Book of Revelation has challenged Christian readers for many centuries. The next eight weeks will be devoted to studying portions of this fascinating book. The first study concerns the introductory words of the writer and his account of the first vision of the book.

▶**Study Aim:** *To describe how John was called to write the Book of Revelation*

STUDYING THE BIBLE

OUTLINE AND SUMMARY

   I. The Revelation of Jesus Christ (Rev. 1:1–8)

      1. Title and blessing (vv. 1–3)

      2. Greeting (vv. 4–5a)

      3. Doxology (vv. 5b–8)

  II. John's Call and Vision of the Son of Man (Rev. 1:9–20)

      1. John, a persecuted exile (v. 9)

      2. John's commission to write (vv. 10–11)

      3. Vision of the Son of man (vv. 12–16)

      4. Message of the crucified, risen Lord (vv. 17–20)

The book is the revelation of Jesus Christ sent and signified to John (vv. 1–3). John greeted the seven churches of Asia in the name of the triune God (vv. 4–5a). John praised Christ, and God declared His future coming (vv. 5b–8). John wrote from the island of Patmos to others who also were being persecuted (v. 9). John heard a voice telling him to write to the seven churches (vv. 10–11). Turning, John saw the Son of man standing in the midst of seven golden lampstands (vv. 12–16). The crucified, risen Lord touched John and confirmed the call to write (vv. 17–20).

I. The Revelation of Jesus Christ (Rev. 1:1–8)

1. Title and blessing (vv. 1–3)

Although the book is often called the Revelation of John, after its human author, the book itself is "the Revelation of Jesus Christ" (v. 1). The divine revelation came to John, who bore witness to what he saw (v. 2). A blessing is pronounced on those who read and obey what is written (v. 3).

2. Greeting (vv. 4–5a)

    4 John to the seven churches which are in Asia: Grace be unto you, and peace, from him which is, and which was, and which is to come; and from the seven Spirits which are before his throne;

5 And from Jesus Christ, who is the faithful witness, and the first begotten of the dead, and the prince of the kings of the earth.

The first line of verse 4 reads like the greeting in most of the letters of the New Testament. John identified himself by name. He apparently was so well known in the Roman province of Asia that they knew which John this was. This was especially true in light of later information about him in verse 9. Early tradition identified the apostle John as living in Ephesus, the chief city of Asia, and thus as the author of the Book of Revelation. "Asia" referred to the Roman province located at the western end of Asia Minor, not to what we know as the continent of Asia. The seven churches are identified in verse 11.

The source of the grace and peace is the triune God. The eternal Creator, God the Father is called the One "which is, and which was, and which is to come." This is reminiscent of His revelation to Moses as the great "I AM" (Exod. 3:14). He had no beginning. He is always at work. He will continue forever.

Although the first line of verse 4 is a familiar style of greeting in New Testament letters, the rest of verse 4 shows that the style of this book will be different from the style of letters. This is especially true of the description of seven Spirits before the throne. The Book of Revelation was written in a style called apocalyptic (uh pahk uh LIP tik), which used symbolic numbers and vivid, sometimes bizarre visions. Many Bible students consider the seven Spirits to represent the Holy Spirit. Seven was considered a number of completion or perfection.

Mentioning the seven spirits between the eternal God and Jesus Christ adds weight to the conclusion that John was referring to the Holy Spirit.

Jesus is described in three ways. He was not a martyr, but He was faithful unto death (Heb. 12:1–4). He was the firstborn from the dead because His victory over death assures victory over death for those who follow Him (1 Cor. 15:20–21). In contrast to the puny Roman emperor who threatened the Christians, Jesus Christ is King of kings and Lord of lords (Rev. 19:16).

3. Doxology (vv. 5b–8)

5 Unto him that loved us, and washed us from our sins in his own blood,

6 And hath made us kings and priests unto God and his Father; to him be glory and dominion for ever and ever.

Amen.

Mentioning the person and work of Christ inspired John to burst forth into praise. The word translated "loved" is in the present tense and means "loves." The word translated "washed" means "loosed" or "freed from." Because Christ loves us, He set us free from our sins through giving His life and shedding His own blood.

The word translated "kings" means "kingdom." Christ made us a kingdom of priests. When God made the covenant with Israel at Mount Sinai, God said, "ye shall be unto me a kingdom of priests" (Exod. 19:6). Peter had the Exodus passage in mind when he wrote that Christians are "a chosen generation, a royal priesthood, an holy nation" (1 Pet. 2:9).

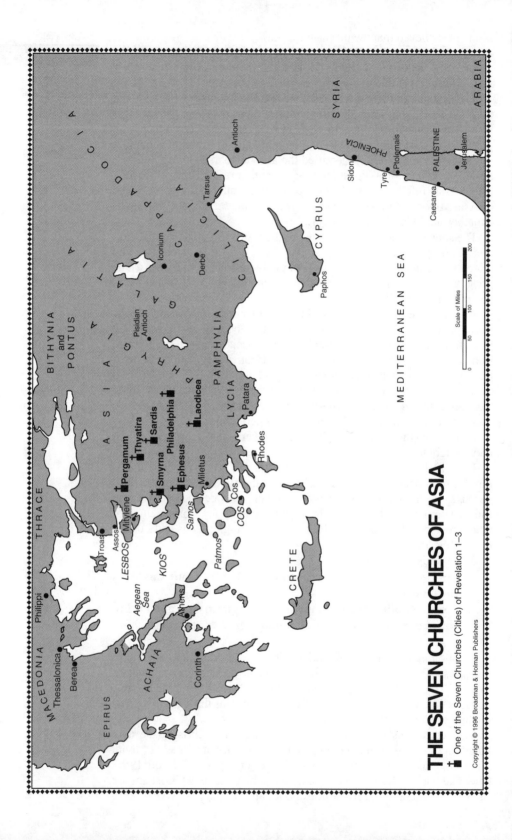

THE SEVEN CHURCHES OF ASIA

✝ One of the Seven Churches (Cities) of Revelation 1–3

Copyright © 1996 Broadman & Holman Publishers

John also believed that the ultimate fulfillment of the Exodus promise is all those who know Christ. When we are brought into God's kingdom, no special group serves as priests. All are priests who offer themselves to God and for one another, and who represent the Lord before the world.

John praised such a wonderful Savior, to whom is given glory and power forever.

7 Behold, he cometh with clouds; and every eye shall see him, and they also which pierced him: and all kindreds of the earth shall wail because of him. Even so, Amen.

The glory and power of Christ will be fully revealed to all people at His coming. Now only believers live in light of His kingdom and coming. When Christ comes, every eye shall see Him. This will include those responsible for His death, as well as all the people of the earth. Believers shall greet His coming with joy, but others will wail because they recognize that they stand under His judgment.

8 I am Alpha [AL fuh] and Omega [oh MEG uh], the beginning and the ending, saith the Lord, which is, and which was, and which is to come, the Almighty.

The One who spoke this prophecy of Christ's coming identified Himself in verse 8. He was none other than Almighty God. He is Alpha and Omega. These are the first and last letters of the Greek alphabet. This means that He is the beginning and the end. God also identified Himself again as the One who is, was, and is coming (as in v. 4). Thus verse 8 is like a divine signature verifying the source of the revelation given to John.

II. John's Call and Vision of the Son of Man (Rev. 1:9–20)

1. John, a persecuted exile (v. 9)

9 I John, who also am your brother, and companion in tribulation, and in the kingdom and patience of Jesus Christ, was in the isle that is called Patmos [PAT muhs], for the word of God, and for the testimony of Jesus Christ.

John identified himself as a brother in Christ and as one who shared with his readers in tribulation, kingdom, and perseverance in Jesus. The word translated "patience" means more than patient waiting; it means actively bearing up under trials. When John received his commission to write, he was on the island of Patmos. This small island off the coast of Asia Minor was used by the Romans as a place of exile for persons guilty of certain crimes. John's "crimes" were his faithful testimony to God's Word and Jesus Christ.

This verse and many others show that the Book of Revelation was written to persecuted believers. Emperor Domitian (doe MISH un), who reigned from A.D. 81 to 96, sought to enforce emperor worship throughout the Roman Empire. The cult of emperor worship had been around for a long time, but most earlier emperors had not taken it too seriously. Domitian was determined that everyone worship the emperor.

For most people of that day, adding one more god to their many gods posed no problem. However, Christians faced a serious dilemma. They were loyal citizens; but their total commitment to Christ would not allow them to say, "Caesar is lord." Instead, they declared, "Jesus is Lord." Their refusal to worship the emperor resulted in various kinds of persecution, including exile in John's case. One key to understanding the Book of Revelation is to read it from the perspective of the persecuted people for whom it was originally written.

2. John's commission to write (vv. 10–11)

10 I was in the Spirit on the Lord's day, and heard behind me a great voice, as of a trumpet,

11 Saying, I am Alpha and Omega, the first and the last: and, What thou seest, write in a book, and send it unto the seven churches which are in Asia; unto Ephesus [EF uh su-hs], and unto Smyrna [SMUR nuh], and unto Pergamos [PUR guh muhs], and unto Thyatira [thigh uh TIGH ruh], and unto Sardis [SAHR diss], and unto Philadelphia [fil uh DEL fih uh], and unto Laodicea [lay ahd ih SEE uh].

While John was caught up in the Spirit on one Lord's Day, he heard a voice that sounded like a trumpet. The Speaker identified Himself, using the language of verse 8. This shows that both God the Father and God the Son were called the Alpha and the Omega. The voice told John to write to seven churches in the Roman province of Asia. The seven churches were named. Revelation 2–3 contain letters addressed to each of the seven churches.

3. Vision of the Son of man (vv. 12–16)

12 And I turned to see the voice that spake with me. And being turned, I saw seven golden candlesticks;

13 And in the midst of the seven golden candlesticks one like unto the Son of man, clothed with a garment down to the foot, and girt about the paps with a golden girdle.

14 His head and his hairs were white like wool, as white as snow; and his eyes were as a flame of fire;

15 And his feet like unto fine brass, as if they burned in a furnace; and his voice as the sound of many waters.

When John turned around, he saw a vision of the exalted Son of man standing among seven golden lampstands. Later Christ identified the lampstands as the seven churches (v. 20). The name "Son of man" and the description of Him clearly show that this was none other than the Lord Jesus Christ. The details of His appearance in verses 13–15 emphasize His purity and His power. This is further seen in verse 16, where He is said to hold seven stars in His right hand, to have a two-edged sword coming out of His mouth, and to have a face that shone like the sun.

The impact of the message was to remind the persecuted believers that Jesus was Lord, not Caesar. They may have wondered whether the Lord knew or cared about their plight. The vision assured them that He was standing with them in the midst of the persecuted churches. This is the central message of the Book of Revelation: The final victory will be Christ's. Meanwhile, believers must remain faithful unto death.

4. Message of the crucified, risen Lord (vv. 17–20)

When John fell down terrified, the Lord laid His right hand on him and told him not to be afraid (v. 17). The Lord said that He had died and was now alive forever, and that He held the keys to death and the grave (v. 18). He told John to write what he had seen, what is, and what will take place later (v. 19). He explained that the seven stars were the angels (or messengers) of the seven churches, and the seven lampstands were the seven churches (v. 20).

APPLYING THE BIBLE

1. Christ's picture in Franklin's room. The religion of Benjamin Franklin was much different from that of the evangelical church. He was a deist who saw God in the world, but that was about all. However, when Franklin was dying he asked for a crucifix, or a picture of Christ on the cross, to be placed in his bedroom so that Franklin could look, as he said, "upon the form of the Silent Sufferer."

John's vision of Christ on Patmos was neither a crucifix nor a picture. John saw the resurrected Christ in all His heavenly glory, and Jesus was real and alive!

2. Christ preeminent. One of Leonardo da Vinci's greatest accomplishments was his painting "The Last Supper." Taking an artist friend along to get his opinion, da Vinci asked his friend what he thought about it. Looking at it carefully, the friend said: "The chalice on the table is remarkably beautiful. In fact, it is the most beautiful thing in the painting." Quickly and deliberately, da Vinci picked up his brush and palette and removed the beautiful chalice. Stunned, the friend asked da Vinci why he had done such a thing. "It is Christ who must be preeminently seen as the center of my painting" da Vinci replied.

Christ is the preeminent person in the Revelation and in all history as well. Look at verses 5, 7–8, 11, 13–18.

3. Christ in history. The massive *Encyclopaedia Britannica* lists the biographies of many great men and women of history. But more words—20,000 words—are used to tell about Jesus than are used for the biographies of Aristotle, Alexander the Great, Cicero, Julius Caesar, or Napoleon Bonaparte. H. G. Wells, the British author of many books, blasphemed and ridiculed Jesus; but when he wrote his famous *Outline of History,* Wells never questioned that Jesus lived and used ten pages to discuss His life.

Christ is in history and Christ is history. He is the Alpha ("A") and Omega ("Z") of all history (v. 11).

4. What Jesus does for sinners. Jesus loves us in our sins (v. 5); He looses us from our sins (v. 5); He lifts us out of our sins (v. 6).

A shepherd who lived in the mountains of Montana had as his only companions a radio, the wild animals and birds, his sheep, his faithful sheepdog, and his beloved fiddle. When his day's work was done, he entertained himself by listening to the radio and playing his fiddle. One day his fiddle got out of tune, and the music went sour. He hit on the idea of writing to the radio station and asking them to sound "A" over the radio at a certain time on a specific day. When the day came, the shepherd was listening carefully, and as the station sounded "A" he tuned his fiddle.

All who tune their lives to the Master bring their lives into harmony with Him as He forgives their sins and lifts them to a higher level of life.

5. To see God walk down the street. Plato, the ancient Greek philosopher, said that he longed to see God walk down the streets of Athens. That is exactly what God did at Bethlehem in Jesus Christ. In the incarnation, God walked down the staircase of heaven to reveal Himself to mankind. We now know what God is like because we have seen Him in Jesus Christ (1 Cor. 1:15). This is what John experienced on Patmos.

TEACHING THE BIBLE

▶ *Main Idea:* Jesus reveals His concern for His people.

▶ *Suggested Teaching Aim:* To lead adults to describe how Jesus revealed His concern for His people to John.

A TEACHING OUTLINE

1. Use a word association test to introduce the Bible study.
2. Use an illustrated lecture to search for biblical truth.
3. Use recall and listing to make the study personal.

Introduce the Bible Study

Give a sheet of paper and pencil to all present. Ask members to number from 1 to 6. Read the following and ask them to write down the first book of the Bible that comes to mind when the word is mentioned: (1) Pastoral instructions, (2) Letter, (3) 666, (4) Beatitudes, (5) Millennium, (6) Antichrist. Allow members to respond and point out that all of the statements except (6) Antichrist are true about the Book of Revelation. In all likelihood, most people chose Revelation for (3), (5), and (6). However, the number *666* and the word "millennium" appear only once in the whole book and the word "Antichrist" doesn't appear at all. It appears only in 1 John and 2 John. Point out that we have let the extraordinary elements of the book overshadow the real meaning. The next eight weeks will help us to discover the real meaning of this book.

Search for Biblical Truth

IN ADVANCE, make a unit poster for the study of Revelation by writing the titles of the lessons, the Scriptures being studied, and the dates on a large poster. Cut out a colored arrow and place this beside the lesson being studied each week.

One of the times when lecture is appropriate is when you have information your members do not have and cannot discover easily. This applies to the lesson this week. **IN ADVANCE,** write the outline on page 2 on poster strips and place them on the wall as you lecture. Place "I. The Revelation of Jesus Christ" and "1. Title and blessing" on the wall. In your lecture point out: the title of the book from 1:1 and the blessing contained in 1:3.

Place "2. Greeting" on the wall. In your lecture: (1) explain who "John" was; (2) locate Asia Minor and the seven churches on a map; (3) explain the source of the grace and peace; (4) define "apocalyptic"; (5) explain the similarities and dissimilarities of the book with other letters; (6) identify the seven spirits; (7) point out the descriptions of Jesus.

Place "3. Doxology" on the wall. Explain: (1) "loved," "washed," and "kings"; (2) that Christ's glory will be revealed when He comes; (3) meaning and purpose of "Alpha and Omega."

DISCUSS: How do I practice my priesthood?

Place "II. John's Call and Vision of the Son of Man" and "1. John, a persecuted exile" on the wall. Then do the following: (1) explain "patience" and locate Patmos on a map; (2) identify Domitian and explain his practice of emperor worship; (3) point out that Revelation was written for people of the first century who were being persecuted.

Place "2. John's commission to write" on the wall. Explain: (1) how and when John received his revelation; (2) who made the revelation; (3) where the seven churches are located on a map.

Place "3. Vision of the Son of man" on the wall. Explain: (1) the lampstands; (2) that Christ's appearance emphasizes His purity and power; (3) that the purpose of the message was to remind believers that Jesus—not Caesar—was in control; (4) that Jesus standing in the midst of the persecuted Christians is the central message of Revelation.

Place "4. Message of the crucified, risen Lord" on the wall. Point out: (1) Jesus is alive; (2) He has the keys to death and hell; (3) the symbols used for the churches.

Give the Truth a Personal Focus

Ask: How does the picture of Jesus revealed in these verses describe His concern for His people? On a chalkboard or a large sheet of paper write members' suggestions. (Possible answers: Jesus stands in the midst of lampstands; Jesus comes to John; Jesus tells John to write this down so others can read it; Jesus' certain victory and return.) Ask: Which of these helps you the most in today's world? Why?

To Smyrna
and Pergamum

Basic Passage: Revelation 2:8–17
Focal Passage: Revelation 2:8–17

Revelation 2–3 contain letters to the seven churches of Asia from the Son of man of the vision of Revelation 1:12–20. This lesson focuses on the letters to Smyrna (SMUR nuh) and Pergamum (PUR guh muhm), which is the usual spelling of Pergamos (PUR guh muhs). The main theme of these two letters and of the Book of Revelation as a whole is the call for God's people to remain faithful unto death in the face of persecution.

▶**Study Aim:** *To state what the letters to Smyrna and Pergamum teach about being faithful to the Lord*

STUDYING THE BIBLE

OUTLINE AND SUMMARY

  I. **Letter to Smyrna (Rev. 2:8–11)**
     1. Greeting (v. 8)
     2. Commendation (v. 9)
     3. Challenge (v. 10)
     4. Promise (v. 11)
  II. **Letter to Pergamum (Rev. 2:12–17)**
     1. Greeting (v. 12)
     2. Commendation (v. 13)
     3. Warning (vv. 14–15)
     4. Challenge (v. 16)
     5. Promise (v. 17)

The crucified, risen Lord greeted the messenger of the church in Smyrna (v. 8). He commended church members for their faithful works and perseverance during persecution and poverty (v. 9). He challenged them to fear not and to remain faithful unto death (v. 10). He promised to those who heeded His word that they would not taste the second death (v. 11). The Lord with the sword coming out of His mouth greeted the church at Pergamum (v. 12). He commended them for faithfulness, even when one of them was killed (v. 13). He warned against the double sin of idolatry and immorality (vv. 14–15). He challenged them to repent (v. 16). He promised them acceptance into God's eternal kingdom (v. 17).

I. Letter to Smyrna (Rev. 2:8–11)
1. Greeting (v. 8)

> **8 And unto the angel of the church in Smyrna write; These things saith the first and last, which was dead, and is alive.**

Each of the seven letters begins with a greeting to the angel of that church. Since the word "angel" means "messenger," many people think

Christ had in mind either the messenger carrying the letter or the pastor of the church. Others think that the "angel" was the guardian angel of the church. In either case, each letter was intended to be read and obeyed by all members of the church.

The sequence of the seven churches in Revelation 2–3 follows a circular route starting north from Ephesus and circling back to Ephesus. Smyrna, which was located on the coast about thirty-five miles north of Ephesus, contained temples to many of the Greek gods.

In most of the seven letters, Christ identified Himself by using descriptions from the vision of Revelation 1:12–20. Thus in verse 8, the exalted Lord used language from Revelation 1:17–18. They were greeted by the One who was crucified and was now alive forever as eternal Lord.

2. Commendation (v. 9)

9 I know thy works, and tribulation, and poverty, (but thou art rich) and I know the blasphemy of them which say they are Jews, and are not, but are the synagogue of Satan.

Persecuted Christians are tempted to doubt that Christ knows or cares about them. Thus the Lord assured the Christians in Smyrna that He knew their tribulation and poverty. He also assured them that He knew of their faithful good works in spite of their troubles. When property is confiscated and jobs are denied to believers, poverty becomes one of the results of persecution. Christ assured them that although they were economically poor, they actually were rich in God's sight (Matt. 6:19–21; James 1:9).

Taking the lead in the persecution in Smyrna were some Jews from the synagogue. Keep in mind that John himself was a Jew, as were all the apostles, and many of the early Christians. Thus this was no indictment of Jews in general, but of those who allowed themselves to become instruments of Satan in trying to destroy those who believed that Jesus is the Son of God. The word "blasphemy," when used against people, means "slander." Thus their opponents stirred up others against Christians by spreading lies about them.

3. Challenge (v. 10)

10 Fear none of those things which thou shalt suffer: behold, the devil shall cast some of you into prison, that ye may be tried; and ye shall have tribulation ten days: be thou faithful unto death, and I will give thee a crown of life.

Although this challenge was addressed to the church in Smyrna, it is repeated in various ways throughout the Book of Revelation. The challenge was twofold: not to be afraid, instead to be faithful unto death. Three reasons were given for being faithful: (1) Regardless of who the human persecutors were, the devil was back of what they did. (2) Although the devil intended persecution to break their faith, God allowed it in order that their faith might be tested and strengthened. (3) Their tribulations would be only for a limited time, but their reward was an eternal crown of life.

4. Promise (v. 11)

11 He that hath an ear, let him hear what the Spirit saith unto the churches; He that overcometh shall not be hurt of the second death.

The first part of verse 11 is found at or near the end of each of the seven letters. The words are similar to the words that Jesus often spoke after saying something that He especially wanted His followers to remember and obey. For example, after telling the parable of the soils, Jesus said, "Who hath ears to hear, let him hear" (Matt. 13:9). The point is that no one has really heard God's word unless hearing leads to obeying. The use of the word "Spirit" in verse 11 shows that the words of the living Christ can be spoken of as the words of the Spirit.

The promise was that those who overcame would never taste the second death. Christ promised no exemption from physical death. In fact, He assured them that remaining faithful could lead to their death as martyrs. His promise was that as believers, they would never face final separation from God, which is the second death (Rev. 20:6,14).

II. Letter to Pergamum (Rev. 2:12–17)

1. Greeting (v. 12)

12 And to the angel of the church in Pergamos write;

These things saith he which hath the sharp sword with two edges.

Pergamum was about fifty-five miles northeast of Smyrna and the northernmost of the seven cities. Not only did it contain temples to Zeus (ZUHS) and other Greek gods, but it also was the site of a great temple dedicated to Rome and Augustus (aw GUHS tuhs) in 29 B.C. This made Pergamum the greatest center of emperor worship in the eastern part of the empire.

The Lord identified Himself using the words of Revelation 1:16. A two-edged sword was a sharp instrument of warfare. In John's vision, Christ had such a sword coming out of His mouth. This signified the power of His word. Hebrews 4:12 uses a similar analogy to describe the power of God's word. Revelation 19:21 pictures Christ doing battle with His evil enemies and slaying them with a sword out of His mouth.

2. Commendation (v. 13)

13 I know thy works and where thou dwellest, even where Satan's seat is: and thou holdest fast my name, and hast not denied my faith, even in those days wherein Antipas [AN tih puhs] was my faithful martyr, who was slain among you, where Satan dwellest.

Christ assured the church in Pergamum that He knew of their faithfulness in the face of persecution. Satan's throne probably referred to Pergamum being the center for emperor worship. The Roman officials in Pergamum took seriously the task of enforcing emperor worship. At least one Christian, Antipas, had lost his life as a result of his faithfulness. Christ commended the church for standing firm during that time.

3. Warning (vv. 14–15)

14 But I have a few things against thee, because thou hast there them that hold the doctrine of Balaam [BAY luhm], who taught Balac [BAY lak] to cast a stumblingblock before the children of Israel, to eat things sacrificed unto idols, and to commit fornication.

15 So hast thou also them that hold the doctrine of the Nicolaitans [nik oh LAY uh tuhns], which thing I hate.

Most of the seven letters include not only commendation but also warning. Although no word of warning was given to the church at Smyrna, Christ warned the church at Pergamum of a serious danger. Although they had overcome the outward pressure of persecution, they were in danger of corruption from within. Verse 14 identifies this as the doctrine of Balaam, and verse 15 calls it the doctrine of the Nicolaitans. Likely, these were two names for the same problem.

Verse 14 identifies the sin as eating things sacrificed to idols and committing sexual immorality. The practice is similar to the snare into which Balaam lured Israel during the period of wilderness wanderings. Balaam was a prophet who was hired to curse Israel by Balak, king of Moab (MOH ab). God restrained Balaam from cursing Israel and led him to speak blessings instead (see Num. 22–24). Numbers 25:1–5 describes how the Israelites offered sacrifices to Moabite gods and committed sexual immorality with Moabite women. Numbers 31:16 shows that Balaam had advised the Moabites to lure the Israelites into these sins (see also 2 Pet. 2:15; Jude 11).

In the ancient world, many religions incorporated sexual immorality as part of their worship. Just as the Israelites often were lured into this double sin of idolatry and immorality, so were Christians tempted to do the same in their day. We don't know exactly the form this took in Pergamum, but verses 14–15 show that the church was condoning and in some cases participating in such sins. The Lord hated such deadly sins.

4. Challenge (v. 16)

16 Repent; or else I will come unto thee quickly, and will fight against them with the sword of my mouth.

Christ's will in such a situation is clear: Repent. He warned the church that unless they repented, He would take direct action against those who practiced, promoted, or condoned these evils. As elsewhere, He said He would go into battle with the sword of His mouth. Verse 16 may have meant that Christ would speak and implement words of judgment against the evildoers. Revelation 19:21 shows that this weapon can destroy all the forces of evil.

5. Promise (v. 17)

17 He that hath an ear, let him hear what the Spirit saith unto the churches; To him that overcometh will I give to eat of the hidden manna, and will give him a white stone, and in the stone a new name written, which no man knoweth saving he that receiveth it.

Many Jews expected the coming of the Messiah to be accompanied by God again providing manna as He had in the wilderness. During His ministry, Jesus claimed to be the Bread of Life (John 6:31–35). The exalted Lord promised to provide satisfying nourishment for His faithful people. They were tempted to join the pagan idol feasts; but if they were faithful, Christ promised that they would eat the hidden heavenly manna.

Victorious athletes were sometimes given a white stone as a ticket of admission to a victory feast and celebration. This may be the meaning of the symbol in verse 17. Faithful Christians were assured of welcome at the heavenly banquet. In some way, each ticket of admission will be personalized. Perhaps this is another sign to teach the same idea as the sign of having one's name written in the book of life (Rev. 20:12).

APPLYING THE BIBLE

1. "Quo vadis, Domine?" There is no statement in the New Testament that Peter was ever in Rome. But Christian writers of the second century developed the tradition that the church in Rome was founded by Peter and Paul. This is wrong, for Paul wrote his epistle to the church in Rome, a church that already existed but which he had never seen (Romans 1:7,11). Also, tradition says that Peter died a martyr's death in Rome, although there is no scriptural evidence to prove or disprove it. According to the tradition, Peter who had been in Rome, was fleeing from the persecution that had broken out within the city. On the road he met a stranger coming into the city. Recognizing that it was Christ, Peter asked, "Quo vadis, Domine?"—"Where are you going Lord?" Jesus answered, "I go to Rome to suffer in your place." Overcoming his fear, tradition relates that Peter turned and went back to Rome, where he suffered a martyr's death.

John's meeting with Jesus on Patmos is fact, not tradition. And Jesus gave John a message to share with the saints who were being persecuted in the seven churches of Asia Minor.

2. Overcoming fear. Dwight L. Moody (1837–1899) was an outstanding evangelist. His favorite verse was Isaiah 12:2: "I will trust and not be afraid." Moody used to say: "You can travel to heaven first-class or second-class. Second-class is, "What time I am afraid, I will trust." First-class is, "I will trust and not be afraid."

John tells these believers that persecution for Jesus' sake will increase but that they should fear none of the things that will befall them, for God always has the last word.

3. Keeping the faith. Eisleben, Germany, is a small inconspicuous town, but an important one nonetheless. At an inn on one end of the town, Martin Luther was born on a night in 1483. At the other end of the town is the house in which he died in 1546. On the night of February 18, 1546, the great reformer awoke in great pain and then sank into a coma. A friend roused Luther and asked, "Reverend father, do you stand firm by Christ and the doctrine you have preached?" In a child's whisper Luther answered, "Yes!"

John writes the suffering believers in the churches to stand by their faith in Christ although it may cost them their lives (v. 10).

4. Repentance required. Theologian Augustus Strong defines repentance as "that voluntary change in the mind of the sinner in which he turns from sin." In all the Bible, repentance is required of all sinners who would be saved.

A man traveling by foot asked a boy along the road how far it was to a certain community. The boy replied: "Mister, if you keep walking the way you are going it is about twenty-five thousand miles. But if you turn around it is about three miles!"

Repentance involves a turning, a change of mind and attitude. The risen Lord, through John, commands the saints at Pergamum to repent. Although they are suffering persecution for Christ's sake, repentance is still required (vv. 14–16). We never arrive at such a high state of holiness that we do not need to repent.

5. Reward waiting. A young man arrived in London and carried his bags down to "the tube" (underground subway) where he was to catch the train to his destination. He boarded the tube, picked up two bags, and was turning around to pick up the other two when suddenly the doors closed and the train sped away. Quickly, he shouted to a man nearby, "Put them out at the Mansion House, please." Then at the next stop, he caught a train back to where his bags were waiting and caught the next train to Mansion House. Sure enough, when he got off the train his two bags were on the platform waiting for him.

What we put in at the cross of Jesus will be waiting for us when we arrive at the Father's mansion house! To the suffering saints at Pergamum, John writes to tell them to be faithful to Jesus, for their reward will be waiting for them when they arrive in heaven (v. 19).

TEACHING THE BIBLE

▶ *Main Idea:* Jesus is with His suffering people.

▶ *Suggested Teaching Aim:* To lead adults to identify ways Jesus has supported them in their suffering.

A TEACHING OUTLINE

1. Use an illustration to introduce the Bible study.

2. Use a chart to guide the search for biblical truth.

3. Use discussion questions to give the truth a personal focus.

Introduce the Bible Study

Share the following illustration: Bill Wallace was a Southern Baptist medical missionary to China before the Communist takeover. He was captured and tortured physically and psychologically. His only crime was having committed his life to heal people physically and spiritually. At night his Communist guards stuck long poles through the bars of his cell and jabbed the doctor into unconsciousness. But something went wrong one night, and the battle was over. "Bill Wallace was dead to the world, but was alive forever with God."[1] Say: Many believers have died for their faith. Today's lesson tells of one of the earliest ones. But more than that, it tells us of Christ's presence in the midst of suffering.

Search for Biblical Truth

IN ADVANCE, make a chart on a large sheet of paper. The chart should have eight columns, and you will use it for the rest of April. Label the columns (1) Church; (2) Attribute of Christ; (3) Condition of the Church; (4) Exhortation; (5) Warning or Commendation; (6) Solemn Refrain; (7) Reward Promised; (8) Title. Leave space beneath to write.

IN ADVANCE, enlist a reader to read all of the Scripture reference. Call for Revelation 2:8–11 to be read at this time. Ask members to fill in (1) the Name of the Church. (Smyrna) and (2) the Attribute from Revelation 1:12–20. ("First and last.") Use a map to locate Ephesus (which will not be covered in this study), Smyrna, and the other five churches (Sardis will not be studied, either).

Ask members to identify (3) the Condition of the Church (v. 9). Use "Studying the Bible" to explain "synagogue of Satan" and "blasphemy." Ask: What assurance does this verse give that Jesus knows and cares about us when we suffer for Him?

Ask members to identify (4) the Exhortation ("Do not fear"); (5) the Warning or Commendation ("Be faithful"); (6) Solemn Refrain (v. 11); and (7) Reward (not hurt by second death). Ask: What three reasons are given for remaining faithful? (See "Studying the Bible.")

Ask members to suggest a title (8). It should be something like *persecuted.*

Call for the reader to read Revelation 2:12–17. Identify Pergamum on the map. Move through the verses and let members fill in the chart. Where appropriate, use "Studying the Bible" to explain the passage.

DISCUSS: What in these verses do you find helpful today? How can you know that Jesus cares about you in your hurt and suffering? What reward do you deserve for your faithfulness?

Give the Truth a Personal Focus

Remind members of Bill Wallace's suffering and death. Point out that although we may not be martyrs for our faith, Jesus is with us when we suffer for Him. Ask: How do we suffer today? (List responses on a chalkboard or a large sheet of paper.) How does Jesus help us today? (List responses.) Why should we be faithful today? (Same three reasons the Smyrna Christians were to be faithful; God has not changed.) Close with a prayer that all will be faithful in the situations in which they find themselves this week.

---

1. Jesse C. Fletcher, *Bill Wallace of China* (Nashville: Broadman Press, 1963, reprint, Broadman & Holman, 1996), 207.

To Thyatira

Basic Passage: Revelation 2:18–29
Focal Passage: Revelation 2:18–29

The longest of the seven letters was sent to the church in Thyatira (thigh uh TIGH ruh), the smallest of the seven cities of Asia. The letter to Thyatira is noted for its words of high praise and stern warning.

▶**Study Aim:** *To explain why Christ spoke words of such high praise and stern warning to the church in Thyatira*

STUDYING THE BIBLE

OUTLINE AND SUMMARY
1. Greeting (v. 18)
2. Commendation (v. 19)
3. Warning (vv. 20–23)
4. Challenge (vv. 24–25)
5. Promise (vv. 26–29)

Christ greeted the church at Thyatira as the Son of God and Judge (v. 18). He commended them for their works, love, faith, service, and perseverance (v. 19). He warned of an evil "Jezebel" who was seducing them to idolatry and immorality (vv. 20–23). He challenged the faithful ones to hold fast until He comes (vv. 24–25). He promised the faithful that they would share in His reign and presence (vv. 26–29).

1. Greeting (v. 18)

18 And unto the angel of the church in Thyatira write; These things saith the Son of God, who hath his eyes like unto a flame of fire, and his feet are like fine brass.

Thyatira was located about forty miles southeast of Pergamum. It was known for its trade guilds. Lydia, whom Paul met in Philippi, had come from Thyatira and was a seller of purple (Acts 16:14). Purple dye was expensive. One of its sources was a root that was plentiful around Thyatira.

The exalted Christ spoke to Thyatira with the deity and authority of the Son of God. He used two descriptions of Himself taken from the vision of Revelation 1:14–15. Both descriptions stress His authority as Judge. Eyes like flames of fire penetrate and consume those guilty of sin. Feet of brass represent the strength and firmness of His judgment.

2. Commendation (v. 19)

19 I know thy works, and charity, and service, and faith, and thy patience, and thy works; and the last to be more than the first.

The word "know" plays a big role in the letters of Revelation 2–3. Christ used this word in each of His commendations (2:2, 9, 13, 19; 3:8) and in two of His warnings (3:1, 15). During times of trouble, Christians are tempted to think that Christ either doesn't know or doesn't care about them. The Lord reminded the believers in the seven churches of Asia that He was among them, that He knew, and that He cared.

The believers at Thyatira were noted for their "works." These were not things they did in order to earn salvation. They were the fruits of a saving knowledge of Jesus Christ. The Son of God used these same words, "I know thy works," to commend some of the other churches, but none received higher praise than Thyatira. Only of them did Jesus say that their last works exceeded their first works. In other words, they had grown in their good deeds and practice of the Christian faith.

The Lord also used other impressive words to describe their growth in good works. For example, their works grew out of self-giving love. "Charity" translates *agape,* the word used for God's love for us and our love as a response to His love. The church at Ephesus had been commended for its works, but the same church was rebuked for having lost its first love (Rev. 2:2–4). The works at Thyatira were rooted in love. Their works also showed their "faith," a word that means trust in God and faithfulness to God. Their works led to acts of service. The word translated "labour" means "service." It refers to acts of love done for others in Christ's name. Christ also commended their perseverance, the meaning of the word translated "patience."

3. Warning (vv. 20–23)

> **20 Notwithstanding I have a few things against thee, because thou sufferest that woman Jezebel [JEZ uh bel], which calleth herself a prophetess, to teach and to seduce my servants to commit fornication, and to eat things sacrificed unto idols.**

The warning to the church at Thyatira was similar to the warning to the church at Pergamum. Both were warned against committing sexual immorality and eating things sacrificed to idols (v. 14). Both warnings used the names of villains from the Old Testament. Pergamum was warned against following people who held the teachings of Balaam, infamous for advising the Moabites to lure Israelites to worship idols and commit sexual immorality (Num. 25:1–4; 31:16). Thyatira was warned against a woman, whom Jesus called "Jezebel." This was probably not the actual name of the dangerous woman in Thyatira, but Christ was saying that she was doing the same things that evil Jezebel had done in her day.

Jezebel was a Sidonian princess who married Ahab, king of Israel. She practiced Baal worship, a fertility religion that combined sexual immorality with its worship. Not content to practice her religion privately, she corrupted Ahab and sought to enforce Baal worship throughout the land of Israel (1 Kings 16:29–33; 18:1–15). Elijah (ih LIGH juh) recognized the deadly danger of Baal worship and challenged Jezebel's prophets to a dramatic contest on Mount Carmel (KAHR mil; 1 Kings 18:16–46).

The exalted Lord warned the church at Thyatira of a woman who was as dangerous to them as Jezebel had been to Israel. The woman claimed to be a prophetess. The Bible mentions other women who were legitimate prophetesses (Exod. 15:20; Judg. 4:4; 2 Chron. 34:22; Luke 2:36;

Acts 21:9). This "Jezebel" only claimed to be a prophetess. If the people of Thyatira applied to her the basic tests of a prophet, they would know she was a false prophet. Deuteronomy 13:1–5 warns against any prophet, regardless of his miracles, who tells people to follow other gods. This woman was claiming special inspiration and authority for her teachings, but her words and deeds showed her to be an instrument of evil.

Some people think that "Jezebel" was an evil woman outside the church, but her claim to be a prophetess and the use of the word "seduce" strongly suggest that she was a member of the church. The church was tolerating her, and some church members were being seduced into following her false teachings and evil practices.

We don't know for sure what she said, but we do know that her advice included idolatry and immorality. Such seduction was probably cloaked in seemingly harmless words. Some Bible students think that the setting was among the many trade guilds in Thyatira. These associations of merchants and workers conducted social gatherings and feasts. Since most people worshiped pagan gods, prayers and sacrifices to pagan gods were included as part of the occasions. Sometimes the celebrations got out of hand and became orgies. Perhaps the so-called prophetess was saying that Christians should participate freely in these celebrations. After all, such participation was good for business and for good relations with the rest of the population.

Very likely, her teaching was an early form of what later was called gnosticism (NAHS tih siz uhm), from the Greek word meaning "know." The Gnostics (NAHS tiks) claimed to have special knowledge withheld from the rank-and-file. Their basic assumption was that anything physical is evil. This led some of them to deny that the Son of God ever truly became flesh. In actions, some Gnostics became ascetics, who tried to deny to themselves any physical pleasures; and others became libertines, who indulged every fleshly appetite.

The latter group reasoned that if the soul is saved, what one does with the flesh doesn't matter. Some Gnostics boasted of their excesses as proof of their great spirituality. Such a view may be implied by the words of verse 24 about knowing "the depths of Satan." This sounds like the boast of someone who claimed that the only way to understand sin is to experience it in every way.

21 And I gave her space to repent of her fornication; and she repented not.

22 Behold, I will cast her into a bed, and them that commit adultery with her into great tribulation, except they repent of their deeds.

23 And I will kill her children with death; and all the churches shall know that I am he which searcheth the reins and hearts: and I will give unto every one of you according to your works.

The Lord had given the woman plenty of opportunities to repent, but she had continued in her evil ways. Now the Lord announced that judgment was at hand. She had sinned in beds of adultery; the Lord was about to cast her into a bed of judgment. The Lord warned all who committed adultery with her. This need not mean that she personally had committed adultery with each of them. It probably means that they followed her example of idolatry and sexual immorality. He warned that they would suffer intensely unless they repented.

Some think that "her children" mentioned in verse 23 referred to children born of her acts of adultery. More likely, "her children" were those who followed her and imitated her actions. Death would be their judgment. These terrible judgments would show not just Thyatira but all the churches that the Lord knows each person's emotions and thoughts as well as actions. More important, it would show that His piercing insight leads to sure judgment on those who think they can get by with sin.

4. Challenge (vv. 24–25)

24 But unto you I say, and unto the rest in Thyatira, as many as have not this doctrine, and which have not known the depths of Satan, as they speak; I will put upon you none other burden.

25 But that which ye have already hold fast till I come.

Verse 24 shows that although some church members in Thyatira had followed "Jezebel," others had not. The commendation of verse 19 and the challenge of verses 24–25 were addressed to the faithful ones in the church. Verse 19 describes them in terms of what they did; verse 24 describes them in terms of what they did not do. They did not follow the teachings of "Jezebel," nor did they participate in her evil deeds. As noted earlier, the evil is described here in language used by the sinners themselves. They boasted of experiencing the "depths of Satan."

Christ had no new challenge for the faithful members of the church. He merely reminded them of what they already knew and were doing. They knew Christ was coming. They knew He had told His people to prepare for His coming by remaining faithful to Him. Thus He reinforced this call to hold fast until He comes.

5. Promise (vv. 26–29)

26 And he that overcometh, and keepeth my works unto the end, to him will I give power over the nations:

27 And he shall rule them with a rod of iron; as the vessels of a potter shall they be broken to shivers: even as I received of my Father.

Christ used Psalm 2:9 as the basis of His first promise to the faithful. This verse is quoted in the New Testament as referring to Christ's coming rule over the nations (Rev. 19:15). Verses 26–27 promise that Christ's people will share in that reign.

The rod of iron was an iron-tipped rod used by a shepherd to guard his sheep. Here it is a sign of the rule of the Shepherd-King and His faithful people. The smashing of earthen pots is another sign of universal sovereignty. Ancient kings often showed their power by smashing clay vessels on which were written the names of subject kings and nations.

28 And I will give him the morning star.

29 He that hath an ear, let him hear what the Spirit saith unto the churches.

Revelation 22:16 refers to Jesus as "the bright and morning star." Like the morning star, Christ provides hope and guidance. Christ thus promised to give them His Spirit as a sign of hope and eventually at His coming to fulfill that hope by His appearing.

APPLYING THE BIBLE

1. "Good-bye, God!" Aaron Burr was vice-president of the United States from 1801 to 1805 under President Thomas Jefferson. Both men were running for the presidency in 1800, but Jefferson won only after the U.S. House of Representatives took thirty-six ballots. On July 11, 1804, Aaron Burr fatally wounded Alexander Hamilton in a duel at Weehawken, New Jersey, and a coroner's inquest found Burr guilty of "willful murder." He was acquitted but his political career was ruined.

A religious revival stirred Princeton University when Aaron Burr was a student. According to a campus tradition, Burr resisted, saying that before the night was over he would decide his relationship with God. Later that night, his fellow students heard Burr fling open the shutters on his window and exclaim loudly, "Good-bye, God!"

There are times we rule God out of our lives, thinking that He doesn't know us and our needs, and if He does know He doesn't care. John reminds the church at Thyatira that God knows all about them and holds them responsible (v. 19).

2. Playing with sin. Several years ago, a newspaper carried the story of Kathy Cramer, of El Toro, California, who was attacked by her "pet" python snake. When she called Monte, the python, to his lunch, it crawled out from under the bed and clamped its jaws on the back of Cramer's neck. She called for her boyfriend, Richard Hull, to help her, but by this time the snake had coiled around Cramer's head and neck. Hull couldn't loosen the snake's grip; so, in desperation, he cut off its head. After having been treated for bites from the nonpoisonous snake, Cramer said: "I'm really sorry we had to kill him because he was a beautiful snake!"

Jesus warns the church about the Jezebel in their midst. Like the Jezebel of the Old Testament who combined worship with sexual immorality, this woman at Thyatira, who claimed to be a prophetess, was teaching things the Lord could not tolerate. The Lord had given her plenty of opportunities to repent, but she refused (vv. 20–23). The occasion served for the risen Lord to warn the church about playing with sin because its consequences are deadly and eternal.

3. A call to faithfulness. One author has written that more believers have died for their faith in the last fifty years than in all recorded history. Although it was difficult to be a Christian in Thyatira, Jesus calls on the saints there "to hold fast till I come."

A strong example of this kind of faithfulness is seen in the life and death of John the Baptist. One of Auguste Rodin's (1840–1917) sculptures is his head of John the Baptist. The head rests on a platter with the hair flowing down nearly covering the ugly scar of the sword. But his mouth is open and his facial muscles are taut as though John were, in death, faithful to his mission, declaring, "I am the voice of one crying" (John 1:23).

Faithfulness is commanded of each of us regardless of the consequences (v. 25).

TEACHING THE BIBLE

▶ *Main Idea:* Believers must do good works and avoid false doctrine.

▶ *Suggested Teaching Aim:* To lead adults to identify good works they will perform.

A TEACHING OUTLINE

1. Use a group writing experience to introduce the Bible study.

2. Use a map to help members locate Thyatira in relation to the other seven cities.

3. Continue to use a chart (see April 13 lesson) to guide the search for biblical truth.

4. Use discussion questions to help apply the Scripture passage.

5. Identify actions members can perform individually or as a group.

Introduce the Bible Study

Place a large sheet of paper on a wall. As members enter ask them to write the name of the Christian they think of first when someone mentions doing helpful things. Begin class by referring to the list and then point out that Jesus highly commended the church at Thyatira for its good works.

Search for Biblical Truth

On a map, locate Thyatira. Ask if anyone can remember someone who came from Thyatira. (Lydia, a seller of purple cloth—Acts 16:14.) Ask members to read silently Revelation 2:18–29. Using the chart started last week, fill in (1) the name of the church and (2) the attribute of Christ from 1:14–15.

DISCUSS: What do you think the reference to Christ's eyes means today?

Ask members to identify (3) the condition of the church. (v. 19.) Point out the importance of the word "know" in these letters. Explain the "works" of the Thyatirans. Point out that works are the fruit of a saving knowledge of Jesus and not a way to earn salvation. Ask: What four words did Jesus use to describe their works? (Love, service, faithfulness, and perseverance.) Point out that Jesus condemns the church as well as commending it. Ask: Why does Jesus condemn Thyatira? (Tolerated Jezebel.) **IN ADVANCE,** enlist a member to read "Jezebel," in the *Holman Bible Dictionary*, page 795, or some other Bible dictionary and give a brief report on Jezebel. Use "Studying the Bible" to explain the possible uses of Jezebel in this letter.

Ask members to fill in (4) exhortation (v. 21), (5) warning or commendation ("cast . . . kill . . . give"—vv. 22–23). Point out the Lord's promise of not putting any other burden on the believers (vv. 24–25).

DISCUSS: Do you believe that God does not put burdens on us that we cannot bear?

Ask members to fill in (6) reward promised (vv. 26–28). Use "Studying the Bible" to explain the promised reward: "rod of iron" and "morning star."

DISCUSS: What meaning do these images have for believers today?

Ask members to fill in (7) solemn refrain (v. 29) and (8) title. A suggested title is *Compromising Church* although members may suggest another title.

DISCUSS: Is compromise always bad? How can we know when to compromise and when to remain firm in our position?

Give the Truth a Personal Focus

Ask members to refer to the names they wrote on the poster at the beginning of class. Ask: What kind of good works did these people perform that you and others found so helpful? What type of good works can you do that would help someone? What criterion for judging our works do you think Christ uses?

Let members suggest actions they can take as individuals and/or as a class. If you choose a class project, select people to help you follow through on the project.

To Philadelphia and Laodicea

Basic Passage: Revelation 3:7–22

Focal Passage: Revelation 3:7–10, 15–21

The letter to the church at Philadelphia (fil uh DEL fih uh) has a warm commendation, but no warning. The letter to the church at Laodicea (lay ahd ih SEE uh) has no commendation, but a strong warning. One thing the letters have in common is Christ's use of "door" as a symbol.

▶**Study Aim:** *To explain Christ's use of "door" in the letters to Philadelphia and Laodicea*

STUDYING THE BIBLE

OUTLINE AND SUMMARY

I. Letter to Philadelphia (Rev. 3:7–13)

    1. Greeting (v. 7)

    2. Commendation (vv. 8–10)

    3. Challenge (v. 11)

    4. Promise (vv. 12–13)

II. Letter to Laodicea (Rev. 3:14–22)

    1. Greeting (v. 14)

    2. Warning (vv. 15–17)

    3. Challenge (vv. 18–20)

    4. Promise (vv. 21–22)

Christ greeted the church at Philadelphia as the holy and true One who alone holds the key to the eternal kingdom (v. 7). He commended the church for its faithfulness and reminded it of the open door set before it (vv. 8–10). Christ challenged the church members to hold fast until His coming (v. 11). He promised to make them pillars in God's temple (vv. 12–13). Christ greeted the church at Laodicea as the Amen, the faithful and true witness, and the source of creation (v. 14). He warned of luke-warmness, pride, and self-sufficiency (vv. 15–17). He challenged them to seek true wealth, righteousness, and insight by repenting and receiving Christ into their hearts (vv. 18–20). He promised that those who over-came would reign with Him (vv. 21–22).

I. Letter to Philadelphia (Rev. 3:7–13)

1. Greeting (v. 7)

> **7 And to the angel of the church in Philadelphia write;**
> **These things saith he that is holy, he that is true, he that hath the key of David, he that openeth, and no man shutteth; and shutteth, and no man openeth.**

Sardis (SAHR diss; Rev. 3:1–6) was about thirty-three miles south-east of Thyatira (thigh uh TIGH ruh), and Philadelphia was about twenty-eight miles southeast of Sardis. Philadelphia was founded in order to spread Greek language and culture to the barbaric tribes beyond it.

Christ addressed the church as the holy and true One. Christ is also the holder of the key of David. Christ came to fulfill God's promise to David of an everlasting kingdom. Jesus Christ and He alone holds the key to entering that eternal kingdom.

2. Commendation (vv. 8–10)

8 I know thy works: behold, I have set before thee an open door, and no man can shut it: for thou hast a little strength, and hast kept my word, and hast not denied my name.

An open door symbolized a God-given opportunity. To what God-given opportunity was Christ referring in verse 8? Some Bible scholars think that He was reinforcing the point He had just made about holding the key of David. In other words, Christ was assuring them of their inclusion in God's eternal kingdom. Because Christ had opened the door and alone had the key, no one could close it.

Many Bible scholars think that Christ was using the open door as a symbol of the missionary opportunity of the church at Philadelphia. Just as the city was founded to spread Greek culture, Christ wanted them to spread the Christian gospel. An "open door" is used several times in the New Testament to describe an opportunity for sharing the gospel (1 Cor. 16:9; 2 Cor. 2:12; Col. 4:3).

The last part of verse 8 speaks of the weakness of the church, but also of their faithfulness in keeping Christ's word and not denying His name. This suggests that they were few in number and had no wealth or prestige. Not many of the early Christians were people of wealth or worldly influence (1 Cor. 1:26–31). Yet their weakness became their strength because it encouraged them to rely solely on the Lord (2 Cor. 12:10).

9 Behold, I will make them of the synagogue of Satan, which say they are Jews, and are not, but do lie; behold, I will make them to come and worship before thy feet, and to know that I have loved thee.

Verse 9 is similar to the words of Revelation 2:9. Although John and most of the original believers were Jews, they and the early Gentile believers faced strong opposition in Asia from some Jews who rejected Jesus as Son of God. John charged that these persecutors were actually instruments of Satan, not of God. The Jews laid exclusive claim to a special covenant of God with Israel. Christ disputed this claim. The true Jews are not those who can trace their ancestry back to Jacob, but people who have faith in the Savior whom God sent for Israel and the whole world (see Matt. 3:9; Rom. 2:28–29; 4:16; Gal. 3:6–7, 28–29).

10 Because thou hast kept the word of my patience, I also will keep thee from the hour of temptation, which shall come upon all the world, to try them that dwell upon the earth.

Because of their faithfulness, Christ promised deliverance from the hour of trial that was coming on the world. Bible students debate whether Christ meant deliverance by providing strength to pass through trials, or deliverance from having to go through trials. Many believers, however, would agree with these two biblical principles: (1) Christ did not exempt

His followers from many of the trials of life, especially the test that comes by being persecuted. However, He did promise to be with them and enable them to be faithful unto death. For example, He said, "In the world ye shall have tribulation: but be of good cheer; I have overcome the world" (John 16:33). Many passages in Revelation and elsewhere speak of Christians going through the trial of persecution.

(2) Christ will punish an unbelieving world. Christians will be exempt from the punishment that God's wrath pours out on a godless world. This seems to be the kind of trial that Christ had in mind in verse 10. This trial is coming on "them that dwell on the earth," a phrase used throughout Revelation to refer to an unbelieving world (Rev. 6:10; 8:13; 11:10; 13:8, 14; 17:8).

3. Challenge (v. 11)

In light of Christ's imminent coming, believers should hold fast what they have.

4. Promise (vv. 12–13)

Christ promised to those who overcame that He would make them pillars in the temple of God, on which would be written the names of God, of the new Jerusalem, and of Christ.

II. Letter to Laodicea (Rev. 3:14–22)

1. Greeting (v. 14)

Christ greeted the church at Laodicea as the Amen, the faithful and true witness, and the source of divine creation.

2. Warning (vv. 15–17)

15 I know thy works, that thou art neither cold nor hot: I would thou wert cold or hot.

16 So then because thou art lukewarm, and neither cold nor hot, I will spue thee out of my mouth.

Christ used the words "I know thy works" to introduce commendations of five churches (2:2, 9, 13, 19; 3:8) and warnings to two churches (3:1, 15). The living Lord walked among His churches and knew what was happening. He knew the faithfulness of some and the unfaithfulness of others. He knew that Laodicea was a lukewarm church. This vivid condemnation communicates to people in every generation. People like some drinks hot and other drinks cold, but no one likes a lukewarm drink. Thus Jesus used a normal human experience to picture the spiritual plight of the church. Just as a person might spit out a tepid, lukewarm drink, so Christ would spit out the lukewarm Laodiceans.

He preferred that they be hot or cold rather than lukewarm. He had rather someone be hot with true zeal than lukewarm spiritually. He would even rather they be cold, like people who have never heard the gospel, than to have heard it and only become lukewarm. People who have not heard might hear and respond with genuine warmth and zeal.

The spiritual meaning of lukewarm is clear. This is a person who has been exposed to the white-hot glow of divine holiness and salvation but has only made a halfhearted response. Such people don't want to run the risks of not being professing Christians and church members, but they don't want to take their faith so seriously that it inconveniences them.

17 Because thou sayest, I am rich, and increased with goods, and have need of nothing; and knowest not that thou art wretched, and miserable, and poor, and blind, and naked:

Prosperity is often a greater test of faith than affliction. God warned Israel about the dangers of wealth, pride, and self-sufficiency after they settled in Canaan (Deut. 8). Laodicea was known for its wealth. Although most of the early Christians elsewhere were poor, this was not the case in Laodicea. Their wealth led them to feelings of pride and self-sufficiency, which are the opposite of feelings of trust and dependence on God.

Jesus had commended the church at Smyrna (SMUR nuh) for being rich although they were poor (Rev. 2:9). He condemned the Laodiceans for being poor although they were rich. They thought they were rich and needed nothing. Christ exhausted the dictionary in using words that described their true plight: wretched, miserable, poor, blind, naked.

3. Challenge (vv. 18–20)

18 I counsel thee to buy of me gold tried in the fire, that thou mayest be rich; and white raiment, that thou mayest be clothed, and that the shame of thy nakedness do not appear; and anoint thine eyes with eye-salve, that thou mayest see.

Laodicea was a banking center, a manufacturing center noted for its spun black wool and a medical center noted for its eye-salve. Christ used these facts to challenge them in three areas of their spiritual lives. They needed a faith that was tested and proved; such would be more precious than gold (1 Pet. 1:7). They needed divine cleansing and righteousness, which was like being clothed in white. They needed real healing and insight, which could only come from total commitment to the Lord.

19 As many as I love, I rebuke and chasten: be zealous therefore, and repent.

Christ made clear that whatever chastening they received was done because He loved them (see Heb. 12:5–11). The Lord's goal was to lead them to repent of their pride, self-sufficiency, and lukewarmness.

20 Behold, I stand at the door, and knock: if any man hear my voice, and open the door, I will come in to him, and will sup with him, and he with me.

This is one of the most familiar verses in the Book of Revelation, and rightly so. It shows that the Lord is not so far away that He must be persuaded to hear us. Instead, He is as near as the entrance to our heart. All we need to do is to hear His voice and open our hearts to Him. Then He will come into our lives and bless us with His presence.

In context, this promise reinforced the call to repent in verse 19. If they repented, Christ would restore full fellowship with them. Thus the promise can apply to those who have drifted from the Lord. But it can also apply to those who have never known the Lord, which could have been the real problem of some in Laodicea.

4. Promise (vv. 21–22)

> **21 To him that overcometh will I grant to sit with me in my throne, even as I also overcame, and am set down with my Father in his throne.**

This verse repeats the promise of Revelation 2:26–27 that believers who overcome will share in Christ's reign. Verse 22 closes this seventh letter with the same admonition found at the end of all the letters.

APPLYING THE BIBLE

1. The narrow way. John Glenn was the first American to orbit the earth in space. In his spacecraft, *Friendship 7*, he circled the earth three times in five hours on February 20, 1962. But reentry into earth's atmosphere to bring Glenn and his spacecraft back to earth was a very critical thing. *Friendship 7* had to reenter through a "corridor" in the earth's atmosphere only seven miles wide. As Glenn reentered, his spacecraft encountered tremendous temperature that began peeling all the "skin" off the spacecraft. If the corridor had been missed, the forces of heat and gravity would have consumed the spacecraft.

Jesus said "strait is the gate, and narrow is the way, which leadeth unto life, and few there be that find it" (Matt. 7:14). To the church at Philadelphia, John identified Jesus as the only One who can open the door to eternal life, for He has the key of David (the kingdom of God—vv. 7–8).

2. Called to be faithful. Roy Angell tells about a spindly boy who was sent in by the coach to represent his school in the mile run. All the other runners came in far ahead of the boy. When the last of the better runners crossed the line, the boy was half a lap behind. Finally, he crossed the line and fell exhausted to the track. The judges rushed out and asked the boy why he didn't quit since he was so far behind. The boy answered: "The coach didn't send me out here to quit, and he didn't send me to win. He sent me to run and I gave it my best!"

Christ doesn't call us to win; He calls us to be faithful (v. 8). We must give Him our best and leave the results up to Him.

3. Love expresses itself. Love is more than a four-letter word. Love works and expresses itself. A promising young doctor graduated from medical school and could have set up a lucrative practice in a large city. Instead, he went to a mountain community where people were poor and the needs were great. Day and night he rode his horse to the homes of the sick and needy. The years and hard work took their toll, and when he died the people gathered to place stones around his grave. Someone remembered his sign which hung at the drugstore. Retrieving the sign, which read, "Office Upstairs," they placed it at the head of his grave. His last act of kindness was to write across each page of his ledger of the people who owed him money, "Paid in full!"

Jesus tells the Philadelphian church, "I have loved thee" (v. 9). That love expressed itself in action at the cross.

4. Backsliders. A minister's little daughter and her friend were talking one day. The little friend, remembering that her pastor had preached on backsliding, asked, "What is a backslider?" The minister's daughter explained that "backsliders don't love Jesus as much as they once did." Continuing, she said, "Once they used to sit up front in church. Then they slide back a row, and they keep sliding until they are on the back row. Soon they don't even come to church at all!"

That's a pretty simple definition of a backslider, but many of us have been guilty of it. The church at Laodica was rebuked by the risen Lord: "I know thy works, that thou are neither cold or hot: I would thou wert cold or hot. . . . I will spew thee out of my mouth" (vv. 15–16).

5. Christ at the door. Revelation 3:20 is one of the best-known verses in Revelation. It is graphically pictured by Holman Hunt's 1854 painting, "Christ as the Light of the World." There stands Christ, knocking on the vine-covered door, waiting to be admitted. But there is no handle on the outside of the door. It represents the human heart that must be opened from within.

Verse 20 shows Christ knocking on the door of the Laodicean church which has, in its lukewarmness, shut Him out. Christ's promise is that if they will repent and open the door to Him, He will come in and fellowship with them.

What a tragedy it is for Christ to be shut out of His church!

TEACHING THE BIBLE

▶ *Main Idea:* God has set before all of us an open door of opportunity.

▶ *Suggested Teaching Aim:* To lead adults to identify opportunities they have as a church and as individuals.

A TEACHING OUTLINE

1. Use a question to introduce the Bible study.

2. Continue to use the chart you started on April 13.

3. Use a poster to help identify opportunities members have as a church and as individuals.

Introduce the Bible Study

Ask: What can doors be used for? Let members suggest ways doors can be used. Say, Jesus referred to doors in His letter to the two churches we study about today. In one, the door is an open door of opportunity; in the other, it is a closed door—one through which Jesus cannot even get in.

Search for Biblical Truth

On a map, locate Philadelphia and Laodicea. Ask members to read silently 3:7–10. Using the chart started April 13, fill in (1) the name of the church and (2) the attribute of Christ from 1:12–18 (key of David).

DISCUSS: What do you think the term "key of David" means?

Fill in the chart for (3) condition of the church ("know thy works . . . not denied my name") and (4) exhortation ("make the synagogue of Satan"). Use "Studying the Bible" to explain possible meanings of "open door."

Fill in the chart for (5) warning or commendation ("I will keep . . . upon the earth"). Point out that Philadelphia is the only church that Christ does not warn. Use "Studying the Bible" to explain interpretations of "keep thee from . . . temptation."

DISCUSS: If Christ were writing our church, would He warn or condemn us? Why?

Although 3:11–13 are not part of the focal passage, quickly fill in the chart for (6) solemn refrain and (7) reward promised. Let members suggest (8) a title (church with opportunity).

Ask members to read silently 3:15–22. Fill in the chart for (1) church and (2) attribute (none).

Ask members to fill in (3) condition of the church ("neither cold nor hot" and "wretched . . . naked"). Ask: How does John indicate that Jesus knew the condition of the church? (Walks in their midst—1:13.) Fill in (4) exhortation (vv. 19–20). Point out that what makes 3:20 so sad is that it is a picture of Christ knocking, trying to get in His church, and they will not let Him in. Fill in (5) warning or commendation (v. 18). Use "Studying the Bible" to explain the background of Jesus' warning to the Laodiceans.

Fill in (6) solemn refrain, (7) reward promised ("grant to sit . . . in his throne"—3:21), and (8) title (consider: "complacent").

DISCUSS: What causes a church that was once strong and vibrant to become a complacent church? What does it take to change? What makes an individual complacent? What does it take to change?

Give the Truth a Personal Focus

IN ADVANCE, on a chalkboard or a large sheet of paper, draw two doors. Over one write *Open* and over the other write *Closed.* Ask: Which "door" would you use to describe our church? your spiritual life?

Point out that all churches and individuals have an open door of opportunity if they will take it. Let members suggest some opportunities they have as a church or as individuals. List these on the "open" door you have drawn. Ask members to choose one or more of these opportunities and plan how they can achieve it.

The Redeeming Lamb

Basic Passage: Revelation 4–5

Focal Passage: Revelation 5:1–10

Following the letters to the seven churches in Revelation 2–3 is a two-fold vision in Revelation 4–5. Revelation 4 pictures the throne of God and all beings praising God. Revelation 5 pictures the Lamb who alone is worthy to open a mysterious scroll and all beings praising Him.

▶**Study Aim:** *To describe what John heard, felt, and saw in Revelation 5:1–10*

STUDYING THE BIBLE

OUTLINE AND SUMMARY

I. Vision of the Holy God (Rev. 4:1–11)
1. The throne in heaven (4:1–3)
2. Beings around the throne (4:4–7)
3. Praises to the holy Creator (4:8–11)

II. Vision of the Lamb (Rev. 5:1–14)
1. The scroll with seven seals (5:1–4)
2. The Lion-Lamb (5:5–7)
3. Worshiping the Lamb (5:8–14)

Called up into heaven, John saw a vision of an awesome throne (4:1–3). Around the throne were twenty-four elders, four living beings, seven lamps of fire, and a sea of glass (4:4–7). After the four beings praised God's holiness, the elders fell down and worshiped Him (4:8–11). John saw the figure on a heavenly throne holding a scroll with seven seals, and John wept because no one was worthy to open the scroll (5:1–4). When an elder told John that the Lion of Judah was worthy to open the scroll, John saw a slain Lamb with seven horns and seven eyes (5:5–7). After the elders and beings praised the Lamb for giving His life to redeem people of every nation, angels joined all creation in declaring the worthiness of the Lamb to receive all glory (5:8–14).

I. Vision of the Holy God (Rev. 4:1–11)

1. The throne in heaven (4:1–3)

A door was opened in heaven, and John was called to come up and see things that shall take place (v. 1). As he was in the Spirit, John saw a throne and someone sitting on it (v. 2). The One on the throne looked like a jasper stone and a sardius, and an emerald rainbow encircled the throne (v. 3).

2. Beings around the throne (4:4–7)

Around the throne were twenty-four thrones on which sat twenty-four elders dressed in white with gold crowns (v. 4). Thunder and lightning came from the throne; and before it burned seven lamps, which are the seven Spirits of God (v. 5). In front of the throne was what looked like a sea of glass; and in the center around the throne were four living creatures (v. 6). The first was like a lion; the second, an ox; the third, a man; and the fourth, an eagle (v. 7).

3. Praises to the holy Creator (4:8–11)

The living creatures sang day and night, "Holy, holy, holy, Lord God Almighty, which was, and is, and is to come" (v. 8). The twenty-four elders fell down and worshiped by casting their crowns before the throne and praising God (vv. 9–11).

II. Vision of the Lamb (Rev. 5:1–14)

1. The scroll with seven seals (5:1–4)

1 And I saw in the right hand of him that sat on the throne a book written within and on the backside, sealed with seven seals.

2 And I saw a strong angel proclaiming with a loud voice, Who is worthy to open the book, and to loose the seals thereof?

3 And no man in heaven, nor in earth, neither under the earth, was able to open the book, neither to look thereon.

4 And I wept much, because no man was found worthy to open and to read the book, neither to look thereon.

North Syrian and Hittite stamp-type seals. Credit: Bill Stephens.

Most of the books of John's day were actually scrolls. The description of this "book" shows that it was a scroll with seven seals and written inside and outside. A Roman law required that seven witnesses affix their seals to a will, thus ensuring its validity. This scroll was not a will, but the seven seals attested to its validity. The writing inside and outside shows that it was full.

The scroll was held out in God's right hand, and the loud voice of a strong angel asked who was worthy to open the scroll by breaking the seals. Apparently at first no one stepped forward, for John reported that no one anywhere was found who was worthy to open the scroll and to reveal its contents. John was devastated by this news. He had come to see what was going to take place. The answer was in the scroll. It appeared that the scroll was going to remain sealed and a mystery.

2. The Lion-Lamb (5:5–7)

A Torah (Genesis-Deuteronomy) scroll being held in its wooden case at a celebration in Jerusalem.
Credit: Bill Stephens.

5 And one of the elders saith unto me, Weep not: behold, the Lion of the tribe of Juda, the Root of David, hath prevailed to open the book, and to loose the seals thereof.

One of the twenty-four elders spoke to John in his sorrow and told him to stop weeping because One was found who could break the seals and open the scroll. He is called the Lion of the tribe of Judah. The lion was a symbol of power and royalty. In Jacob's final blessings to his sons, he called Judah "a lion's whelp" and foretold the coming of Shiloh (Gen. 49:9–10). The Lion was also called the Root of David. This reflects another messianic prophecy in Isaiah 11:1–10, which describes One who is the root of Jesse, David's father. These two prophecies were part of the promise of a Messiah who would fulfill God's promises to David and reign with royal power.

The elder told John that this King was worthy to open the scroll because he "hath prevailed." The word means to overcome or be victorious. It is the same word that the Lord used in challenging the seven churches to overcome in the face of persecution (2:7, 11, 17, 26; 3:5, 12, 21). More is revealed in verses 6–10 about the kind of victory He won.

6 And I beheld, and, lo, in the midst of the throne and of the four beasts, and in the midst of the elders, stood a Lamb as it had been slain, having seven horns and seven eyes, which are the seven Spirits of God sent forth into all the earth.

The elder had told John that a Lion was worthy to open the scroll; but when John looked, he saw a Lamb. The Lamb was alive and standing, but it showed evidence of having been slain. The Lamb was the Lamb of God who takes away the sin of the world (John 1:29). The Old Testament background included the Passover lamb that was killed to deliver the Israelites from the death angel (Exod. 12:1–16). Even more significant is the prophecy of the Suffering Servant in Isaiah 53. The Servant was "brought as a lamb to the slaughter" (Isa. 53:7), but He went voluntarily to offer Himself for the sins of others. Philip told the Ethiopian that this prophecy was fulfilled in Jesus (Acts 8:30–35).

These two strains of Old Testament prophecy—the coming King and the Suffering Servant—came together in Jesus Christ. During His earthly ministry, Jesus was cautious about accepting the title of King. He knew that many had a purely earthly image of what the Messiah was to do (John 6:15). Even His disciples did not understand Jesus' words about the necessity of suffering and dying (Matt. 16:21–23; Mark 9:32). When Jesus died, His followers thought of His death as a defeat. Only in light of His Resurrection did they see that the cross and Resurrection won the victory of the Lion-Lamb over sin, death, and Satan. Other kings seek to win victories by force of arms; this Lion-Lamb won the victory by giving Himself for others.

The slain Lamb had seven horns and seven eyes, which are the seven Spirits of God. Horns, like lions, were a symbol of royal power. Most Bible students believe that the seven Spirits signify the Holy Spirit. The seven spirits are the eyes of Christ in the world. The Gospel of John describes the Holy Spirit sent forth into the world to convict of sin and to exalt Christ (14:26; 15:26; 16:7–15). The Book of Acts describes Christ continuing His work in the world through the Holy Spirit (Acts 1:1–8).

During the Middle Ages, some painters sought to capture the scene by painting a slain lamb with seven horns and seven eyes. Christians readers of the first century knew that the vision signified Jesus Christ, the Lamb of God. The reality was not an actual lamb with seven horns and seven eyes. The reality was what that signified. Keep this in mind as you read other strange visions described by John. In other kinds of literature, the words describe the reality in straightforward terms. In prophetic visions, the reality is often not the sign itself, but something that the sign pointed to.

> **7 And he came and took the book out of the right hand of him that sat upon the throne.**

In a dramatic move the slain Lamb went to the throne where God was holding the scroll in His right hand. The force of "took" is as if the wording were, "He went up and took it, and now He has it."

3. Worshiping the Lamb (5:8–14)

> **8 And when he had taken the book, the four beasts and four and twenty elders fell down before the Lamb, having every one of them harps, and golden vials full of odours, which are the prayers of saints.**

Who were the twenty-four elders? Some Bible students think that they and the four living beings were angelic orders around God's throne. Many think that the elders represented the redeemed people of God, who are described in the song of verses 9–10. The new Jerusalem is described as having twelve gates named for the tribes of Israel and twelve foundations named for the apostles (Rev. 21:12, 14). Therefore, could the twenty-four elders be Old and New Testament believers? Some Bible students think that the twenty-four elders represent the church that had been raptured and that much of the rest of Revelation describes events of the Great Tribulation.

The twenty-four elders worshiped the Lamb by falling down before Him.

Each elder had a harp for praise in song, and golden vials which represented the prayers of the saints. Christians are sometimes tempted to believe that their prayers are not heard. First-century believers were being persecuted. They prayed for the Lord to come. However, their persecutors continued their evil work and the Lord continued to delay His coming. John's vision assured him and other persecuted believers that their prayers were like incense that goes up before God and Christ. Such prayers are heard and answered in God's way and in God's time.

9 And they sung a new song, saying, Thou art worthy to take the book, and to open the seals thereof: for thou wast slain, and hast redeemed us to God by thy blood out of every kindred, and tongue, and people, and nation;

10 And hast made us unto our God kings and priests: and we shall reign on the earth.

The redeemed of God sang a new song declaring that the Lamb was worthy because He had redeemed them and made them a kingdom of priests. Slaves could be set free by the payment of a redemption. By His death, Jesus set us free from sin and death by purchasing us with His own blood. The redeemed come from all nations, languages, and people groups, not just from the Jews.

As in Revelation 1:6, the word "kings" means "kingdom." The background is Exodus 19:6, where God promised to make Israel "a kingdom of priests, and an holy nation." The New Testament cites this verse as fulfilled in all God's people in Christ (see 1 Pet. 2:9). In a sense, God's kingdom has already come; and Christ and His people already reign. However, this is apparent only through eyes of faith. When the kingdom comes, Christ will reign; and He will share His reign with His people (Rev. 2:26–27; 3:21; 20:6).

Millions of angels around the throne and the four living beings joined with the twenty-four elders to praise the Lamb as worthy of all glory (vv. 11–12). They in turn were joined in praise to the Lamb by all creatures in heaven, and on earth, and under the earth (v. 13). The four living beings said, "Amen"; and the twenty-four elders fell down and worshiped Him that lives forever and ever.

APPLYING THE BIBLE

1. We can never know all about God. British author H. G. Wells (1866–1946), in his novel *The Soul of a Bishop*, tells about a conversation a bishop had with an angel. Discussing the greatness of God, the bishop said, "But the Truth; you can tell me the Truth." Smiling, the angel cupped his hands over the bishop's bald spot, stroked it affectionately, and said: "Truth! Yes, I could tell you the Truth, but could this hold it? Not this little box of brains. You haven't things to hold it with inside this."

Although John labors in 4:1–7 to describe God's glory and majesty, John barely touches the truth about God's nature, character, and glory. Jesus reveals the Father to us, but still we can never know all there is to know about God.

2. Praise spontaneous. An elderly woman dearly loved her Lord, and during her pastor's sermons she would frequently shout, "Praise the Lord!" When she shouted he would lose his line of thought in his sermon. He spoke to her about it one day, and she promised to contain her emotions. For a while she did well, but one day a visiting preacher was preaching on the forgiveness of sin, and "Aunt Mary" cut loose with one of her "Praise the Lord" shouts. Later, she confided to her pastor, "promise or no promise, I just couldn't help but praise the Lord for He has forgiven all my sins."

Verse 8 shows the spontaneous praise to God of the heavenly being. Seeing His glory and majesty, they cry out day and night, "Holy, holy, holy, Lord God Almighty, which was, and is, and is to come."

God expects and commands us to praise Him for it is pleasing to Him (see the Psalms). It is a natural thing for the believer to praise his God, but we do all too little of it.

3. Who knows the future. There is a craze in the world today about psychics and astrologers. And almost every newspaper in the nation daily carries the astrology charts. This is an abomination to the Lord (Mic. 5:12). Our future is not to be found in the pagan study of the stars; it is found in Jesus Christ, the star of David, the Bright and Morning Star (Rev. 22:16; 2 Pet. 1:19). Only He can unlock for us the future (5:1–7).

4. Christ the key. Lewis Carroll is famous for his children's story *Alice in Wonderland*. In one of his other stories, Carroll tells about an animated padlock. Alive, then, with spindly legs and arms, the padlock is in great distress. When another character in the story asks the padlock what is wrong it replies, "I am seeking for the key to unlock myself!"

When the angel asked, "Who is worthy to open the book, and to loose the seals thereof?" Jesus stepped forward to open the book (5:7). Only Jesus knows the future.

5. He only said, "I love you." Several years ago the newspaper carried the sad story of five-year-old Jeffrey Lansdown, who was beaten to death by his father. His mangled body was found at the bottom of an embankment near a desert road. For three weeks before his murder, little Jeffrey had suffered unmercifully at the hands of his crazed father. The mother later said she did not intervene because she was afraid the father would hurt her and their other children.

After Jeffrey's body was discovered, the police asked his mother what Jeffrey said when his father had threatened to kill him. Sobbing, the mother replied, "Jeff only said, 'Daddy, I love you.'"

That's all Jesus said when they nailed Him to the cross. Jesus still bears the marks of His love for us in His risen, glorified body. John sees Jesus as "a Lamb as it had been slain" (5:6, 9). Our redemption is an eternal cost to Jesus. And all he said was "I love you!"

TEACHING THE BIBLE

▶ *Main Idea:* Jesus alone is worthy because He was crucified and resurrected.

▶ *Suggested Teaching Aim:* To lead adults to worship Jesus because of who He is and what He has done for us.

A TEACHING OUTLINE

1. Use a thought question and a hymn to introduce the Bible study.

2. Use Scripture search and group discussion to search for biblical truth.

3. Plan a brief time of worship to conclude the lesson and to honor Christ.

Introduce the Bible Study

Ask members if they remember the one symbol that tied both of the letters to Philadelphia and Laodicea together. (Door.) Ask them to look at 4:1. Ask: How is the door used in this verse? (The scene of revelation shifts from earth to heaven; John sees into heaven through the door.)

IN ADVANCE, enlist a member to read the hymn, "Holy, Holy, Holy." Then ask members to skim Revelation 4 and see how many references to the hymn they can find in this chapter. Point out that this sets the stage for the rest of the book.

Search for Biblical Truth

Ask members to read 5:1–4 silently. Ask: What did the angel ask? (For someone worthy to open the scroll.) What was John's reaction? (Wept because no one was found who could open the scroll.)

Ask members to read 5:5–7. Ask members to identify the terms used to describe Jesus. (Lion, Root, Lamb.) Using "Studying the Bible," lecture briefly on the following points: (1) the significance and background of each of the three names; (2) the relationship between the royalty of Jesus and the Suffering Servant; (3) the meaning and significance of the seven horns, eyes, and spirits; (4) the reality of the vision was not an actual lamb but what the lamb signified.

Ask members to read 5:8–10. Ask: Who were the twenty-four elders? (See "Studying the Bible" for options.) What message in verse 8 did these elders communicate to first-century Christians and hence to us? (Prayers were like incense that went to God; God heard and received all the prayers.) What did the elders announce? (Jesus was worthy to open the scroll.)

Ask volunteers to read: (1) Exodus 19:6 (point out that this verse is set in the context of God giving the Ten Commandments on Sinai—Exod. 20); (2) 1 Peter 2:9; (3) Revelation 1:6 (preferably in a translation that uses "kingdom" instead of "kings").

Ask: What does it mean to be a "kingdom of priests"? How do we demonstrate our priesthood toward ourselves? toward others? toward Christ?

DISCUSS: How important is the concept of the priesthood of the believer to you? Why?

Give the Truth a Personal Focus

Read the "Suggested Teaching Aim: To lead adults to worship Jesus because of who He is and what He has done for us." Ask: What has Jesus done for you? What have you done for Him? Suggest that one aspect of the Old Testament priesthood was to lead in worship. As New Testament priests, we, too, are to worship and praise Jesus. Read or sing the words to "Holy, Holy, Holy" as a concluding praise.

Provision for
the Redeemed

Basic Passage: Revelation 7:1–17

Focal Passage: Revelation 7:1–3, 9–10, 13–17

Revelation 7 records two visions. Revelation 7:1–8 pictures 144,000 servants of God who receive the seal of divine protection. Revelation 7:9–17 pictures a great multitude of the redeemed serving before the throne of God.

▶**Study Aim:** *To describe the two visions in Revelation 7*

STUDYING THE BIBLE

OUTLINE AND SUMMARY

    I. **Vision of 144,000 Sealed Servants of God (Rev. 7:1–8)**

        1. Seal of the living God (vv. 1–3)

        2. The 144,000 (vv. 4–8)

    II. **Vision of a Multitude of the Redeemed (Rev. 7:9–17)**

        1. A great multitude (vv. 9–12)

        2. Their identity (vv. 13–14)

        3. Their destiny (vv. 15–17)

John saw four angels holding back the four winds and another angel with the seal of the living God (vv. 1–3). He heard that 144,000 servants were sealed, 12,000 from each tribe of Israel (vv. 4–8). He saw a great multitude from all nations clothed in white and holding palms, and he heard their cry of praise for salvation to God and the Lamb (vv. 9–12). When John told one of the elders that he didn't know who they were, the elder told him that they were those out of great tribulation who had washed their robes in the blood of the Lamb (vv. 13–14). They serve before God's throne, enjoy His eternal presence, and are exempt from the blights of earthly life (vv. 15–17).

I. Vision of 144,000 Sealed Servants of God (Rev. 7:1–8)

1. Seal of the living God (vv. 1–3)

    1 And after these things I saw four angels standing on the four corners of the earth, holding the four winds of the earth, that the wind should not blow on the earth, nor on the sea, nor on any tree.

    2 And I saw another angel ascending from the east, having the seal of the living God: and he cried with a loud voice to the four angels, to whom it was given to hurt the earth and the sea,

    3 Saying, Hurt not the earth, neither the sea, nor the trees, till we have sealed the servants of our God in their foreheads.

Revelation 6 provides the background for this vision. Six of the seven seals were opened. The opening of the sixth seal led to an outpouring of divine wrath. The rulers on earth said that "the great day of his wrath is come; and who shall be able to stand?" (v. 17). Revelation 7 answers that question.

The seventh seal of the scroll (Rev. 5) had not yet been broken. Thus the scroll still remained sealed. Before it was opened and God's final wrath was described, the two visions of Revelation 7 were presented as assurances to the people of God. Before God's wrath fell, four angels appeared. They were holding back the four winds so that the winds might not blow on the earth, the sea, or any tree.

Then another angel came from the east with the seal of the living God. He commanded the four angels not to hurt the earth, the sea, or any tree until God's servants could be sealed on their foreheads. This is a picture of restrained judgment and of divine protection for God's servants.

A seal in the ancient world referred to an impression made by a seal of a person's identity and authority. The seal was affixed to documents to show their authenticity and authority. Today we would use a notarized or guaranteed signature. Ancient kings often used a signet ring as their seal. Pharaoh gave Joseph such a ring (Gen. 41:42). The stone of the lion's den in Daniel 6:17 was sealed with the signet rings of the Persian king and nobles.

The Old Testament background to Revelation 7:1–3 was the blood of the lamb over the doors of the Israelites during the final plague on Egypt. The death angel passed over their homes when he visited death on the firstborn of each house without the blood (Exod. 12:23). In the same way, the sealing of God's servants in Revelation marked them as belonging to God and thus exempt from His judgments on the ungodly.

Another New Testament reference to sealing is the revelation that believers have been sealed with the Holy Spirit unto the day of redemption (Eph. 4:30). The Spirit is a divine pledge of our final redemption (Eph. 1:13; 2 Cor. 1:22).

2. The 144,000 (vv. 4–8)

The servants of God who were sealed numbered 144,000, with 12,000 from each of the twelve tribes of Israel.

II. Vision of a Multitude of the Redeemed (Rev. 7:9–17)

1. A great multitude (vv. 9–10)

9 After this I beheld, and, lo, a great multitude, which no man could number, of all nations, and kindreds, and people, and tongues, stood before the throne, and before the Lamb, clothed with white robes, and palms in their hands;

10 And cried with a loud voice, saying, Salvation to our God which sitteth upon the throne, and unto the Lamb.

In this vision, John saw a great multitude too numerous to count. They were from every language, nation, and people group. They were standing before the throne described in Revelation 4–5. They were clothed in white robes and held palms in their hands, and they praised God and the Lamb for divine salvation.

The white robes are explained in verse 14. The palms were signs of God's deliverance and care. The background was the Feast of Tabernacles, which celebrated God's deliverance of Israel from Egypt and His care of them in the wilderness (Exod. 12–18; Lev. 23:39–43; Neh. 8:14–17). Thus the great multitude stood before the throne of God and loudly declared the salvation of God and the Lamb.

In another link with the visions of chapters 4–5, the angels, elders, and living beings around the throne worshiped God with lavish words of praise (vv. 11–12).

2. Their identity (vv. 13–14)

13 And one of the elders answered, saying unto me, What are these which are arrayed in white robes? and whence came they?

14 And I said unto him, Sir, thou knowest. And he said to me, These are they which came out of great tribulation, and have washed their robes, and made them white in the blood of the Lamb.

As in Revelation 5:5, one of the twenty-four elders around the throne of God spoke to John. The elder asked him two questions: Who are these clothed in white robes? Where do they come from? The Book of Revelation has many similarities to the Book of Ezekiel. When the Lord showed Ezekiel the vision of dry bones, God asked the prophet, "Can these bones live?" to which the prophet replied, "Thou knowest" (Ezek. 37:3). John made the same humble reply to the elder. Neither Ezekiel nor John presumed to know the answer to the questions until it was revealed to him.

The elder identified the multitude clothed in white as those who had washed their robes white in the blood of the Lamb. The gospel song "Are You Washed in the Blood of the Lamb?" correctly interprets the meaning of Revelation 7:14. The blood of the Lamb provides salvation from sins. When sinners repent of their sins and trust Christ as Lord and Savior, their lives are cleansed and they are forgiven of their sins. Paul wrote of Jesus Christ, "We have redemption through his blood, the forgiveness of sins, according to the riches of his grace" (Eph. 1:7). In the introductory words of Revelation, John praised Christ who "loved us, and washed us from our sins in his own blood" (Rev. 1:5).

The elder also explained that the great multitude were "they which came out of great tribulation." In discussing a similar promise in Revelation 2:10, we differentiated between tribulation as punishment from God and tribulation as persecution of Christians by ungodly people. The comment was made that believers are exempt from the former, but not the latter. The coming of the white-robed throng "out of great tribulation" is understood by some Bible students to mean that they were delivered from the divine wrath to be visited on the ungodly. Others understand the meaning to be deliverance through persecution. In other words, these were those who overcame and won the victory through a perseverance that was rooted in preservation by the Lord.

3. Their destiny (vv. 15–17)

15 Therefore are they before the throne of God, and serve him day and night in his temple: and he that sitteth on the throne shall dwell among them.

16 They shall hunger no more, neither thirst any more; neither shall the sun light on them, nor any heat.

17 For the Lamb which is in the midst of the throne shall feed them, and shall lead them unto living fountains of waters: and God shall wipe away all tears from their eyes.

The multitude of the redeemed were standing before the throne of God, which was described in chapters 4–5. They are described as serving God day and night in His temple. This shows that the future life of the redeemed is not a dull, useless existence. Instead, the redeemed shall serve the Lord. The Bible does not describe all the forms that this service will take, just as it does not try to explain to earthbound minds all of the glories of the future. Knowing the redeemed will serve Him is enough for now.

The central reality of future blessedness is that God Himself shall dwell with His people. The heart of Christian hope focuses not on ourselves and our survival, but on God and His glorious purpose and presence. Believers in every generation seek God's presence through faith now and confidently hope for His full and eternal presence when God's kingdom comes.

Because God abides with His people, those things that have blighted earthly life will be no more. This is one way the Bible does seek to communicate to us the glory of heaven—by telling us the things that will not be there. The elder revealed to John that the white-robed multitude would not hunger or thirst any more. The burning sun and stifling heat will be no more. The Lamb, who shed His blood for redemption, was described as the Good Shepherd. He shall feed and lead the redeemed unto living springs of water. Like some other parts of verses 15–17, the final promise of verse 17 foreshadows the later description of the new heaven and new earth in Revelation 21:1–22:5.

As in other parts of the Book of Revelation, Bible students agree about some things in chapter 7, and disagree about others. The Book of Revelation was written in a prophetic style called apocalyptic (uh pahk uh LIP tik) literature. The meaning is not presented in the straightforward manner as in biblical narratives, letters, and laws. The symbols of apocalyptic literature are subject to a variety of interpretations.

Some Bible students identify everything after Revelation 4:1 as taking place after a secret rapture of the church. They see the 144,000 as Jews converted during a seven-year tribulation. They see the great multitude as Gentiles converted by the testimony of believing Jews. These tribulation saints then serve in a restored temple during the thousand-year reign (Rev. 20:1–10), called the millennium.

Other Bible students identify the 144,000 sealed servants of God as the same people described as a great multitude of redeemed people. The difference between the groups is not that one was Jewish and the other was Gentile. The difference is that verses 1–8 describe the redeemed on earth, and verses 9–17 describe them in heaven. The number 144,000 is a symbolic way of describing all God's people. According to this view, the sealing of the 144,000 servants shows that God will guard and preserve His people through earthly tribulations. The praises of the white-robed multitude signify the certainty of final salvation into eternal life for God's redeemed people.

In spite of these disagreements, nearly everyone agrees that both groups represent God's redeemed people who are saved by grace through faith. The two visions communicate assurance to people of faith that God protects them and that they shall share a future glory beyond human description.

APPLYING THE BIBLE

1. The judgment to come. The county sheriff was an honest, moral man but he was not a Christian. A pastor in the community was concerned about the sheriff's salvation and urged him to trust Christ as his Savior. The aggravated sheriff replied, "I am not afraid to die." He said he refused to be scared into "religion." But the pastor persisted, telling the sheriff that judgment and eternity lay beyond the grave. The pastor's words got through to the sheriff's heart; and he said that although he was not afraid to die, he trembled when he thought of the judgment to come.

Our lesson today speaks about the coming judgment of God against the wicked, but it also reveals that the believer shall be protected by the grace of God in that judgment day (vv. 1–3).

2. Marked by the blood. G. Campbell Morgan (1863–1945), the well-known British preacher, crossed the Atlantic fifty-four times in his evangelistic ministry. Once, when he was preaching to the "down-and-outs" in a mission, an old, gaunt rag picker came down the aisle and knelt at the altar. Campbell spoke to him about the blood of Jesus that cleanses us from all our sins. Next to the old beggar knelt the mayor of the city; and Morgan told him, too, about the cleansing blood. Campbell said he knew that sometime ago the mayor had sentenced the old rag picker to a month at hard labor and that the man had only recently gotten out of jail.

When the men arose from their knees, the mayor said, "Well, we didn't meet here last time," and the old beggar replied, "No, we will never meet again like we did the last time, praise God!"

As the Israelites were marked by the blood when the death angel passed over Egypt, so every believer in Christ is changed and marked by Christ's blood when he or she turns in faith to Christ (v. 3).

3. The conversion of B. H. Carroll. B. H. Carroll was the founder of Southwestern Baptist Theological Seminary, in Fort Worth, Texas. Although he had been baptized as a child, young Carroll said he wasn't a Christian. Wounded at the Battle of Mansfield, Louisiana, in the Civil War, Carroll returned home to Caldwell, Texas, avowing that he had turned himself "over to infidelity." At the age of twenty-two he vowed never to enter a church again. Carroll's mother, however, persuaded him to attend a Methodist camp meeting one morning in the fall of 1865. Returning to the meeting that evening with his brother, Carroll made a profession of his faith in Christ, and the infidel became a preacher. For almost fifty years Carroll served Christ faithfully and powerfully, and his influence continues to this day.

In his vision on Patmos, John saw "a great multitude" out of all nations who were "clothed in white robes" (v. 9). They were praising

God and saying, "Salvation to our God which sitteth upon the throne, and unto the Lamb" (v. 10).

Jesus saves and cleanses sinners without regard to standing, race, or sinfulness. As he saved Carroll, the infidel, so will he save all who come to him in faith.

4. Answering heaven's roll call. An anonymous poet wrote:

> Traveler, what lies over the hill?
> Traveler tell to me;
> I am only a child—from the window sill
> Over which I cannot see.

What lies over "the hill" for the believer? More than we can ever dream! British author William Thackeray tells about old Colonel Newcome, who was bedridden. Just before he died, Newcome heard the bells in the nearby school chapel tolling the hour. The old colonel's hands were outside the covers, and his feeble fingers beat the time as the bell rang. With the last ring, he said, barely above a whisper, "Adsum." That was the Latin word meaning "present" that they answered in the school of his boyhood days when the teacher called the roll.

One of these days Jesus will call the roll in heaven. What will heaven be like? We don't know a great deal about heaven, but John describes some of its glories in verses 15–17.

TEACHING THE BIBLE

▶ *Main Idea:* God's presence with His people assures them of protection and a future glory beyond human description.

▶ *Suggested Teaching Aim:* To lead adults to describe the assurance God offers to His people.

A TEACHING OUTLINE

1. Use an open-ended sentence to introduce the Bible study.
2. Use a lesson poster to guide the Bible study.
3. Use lecture and questions to search for biblical truth.
4. Use summarizing to identify God's assurance.

Introduce the Bible Study

On a chalkboard or a large sheet of paper write: *Heaven is a place where . . .* As members enter, ask them to write their response to the sentence on the board or a sheet of paper. Begin by reading their responses. Say: The lesson today will describe some of what heaven is like.

Search for Biblical Truth

Make a lesson poster by copying the outline on page 39. Cover all the points until you are ready to teach them.

Uncover the first main point and the first subpoint on the poster. Briefly set the context of this chapter by explaining the following from

"Studying the Bible": (1) Revelation 7 answers the question in 6:17; (2) the two visions in chapter 7 were presented as assurances to God's people before His final wrath fell; (3) how seals were used in the ancient world; (4) the Old Testament background (Exod. 12:23) of Revelation 7:1–3; (5) the purpose of the sealing of God's servants was to mark them as belonging to God and exempt them from His judgments on the ungodly.

Uncover the second subpoint on the outline and state that those sealed were 12,000 from each tribe, symbolizing all of the people on earth who were believers.

Uncover the second major outline point and the first subpoint under it. Ask members to find words in verse 9 that describe this multitude. (So many they could not be counted; from every nationality, race, and language; clothed in white and carried palm branches.) Ask: What were they doing? (Praising God for His salvation.) What do the palm branches remind you of? (Possibly Jesus' royal entry into Jerusalem; the Feast of the Tabernacles which celebrated God's deliverance of Israel from Egypt and His care of them in the wilderness (Exod. 12–18; Lev. 23:39–43; Neh. 8:14–17).

Uncover the second subpoint on the outline. Ask: What two questions did the elder ask John? (Who are these, and where do they come from?) What was the elder's response? (The multitude are those who had been cleansed by the blood of the Lamb and who had come out of the tribulation on earth.)

Use "Studying the Bible" to explain the two interpretations of "came out of great tribulation": (1) those who had escaped the tribulation because of God's deliverance or (2) those who had passed safely through it and had survived it.

Uncover the third subpoint on the outline. Ask: What do the redeemed do in heaven? (Serve God.) What will be the relationship of God to the redeemed? (God will dwell with His people.) What will heaven be like because of God's presence? (No hunger, thirst, burning heat; the Lamb will provide food and water for the redeemed; God will remove everything that causes sadness.)

Use "Studying the Bible" to explain two of the interpretations of this chapter: (1) events taking place after a secret rapture of the church or (2) events that depict the redeemed on earth and also in heaven. You may want to present both views as described in "Studying the Bible" so members can make up their minds.

Give the Truth a Personal Focus

Ask members to think about the chapter and to express in one word what the chapter says to believers of the first century and to us. (Their choice, but consider: assurance.) Ask members to identify statements from this chapter that give them assurance. Challenge all members to be certain they are a part of the redeemed so they can experience God's presence and all that involves.

The Victorious Christ

Basic Passage: Revelation 19–20

Focal Passage: Revelation 19:11–16; 20:11–15

Revelation 19–20 contain many powerful images of Christ as Victor. Volumes have been written about each of the various images, especially Revelation 20:1–10. This lesson will focus on two visions: Christ coming as Victor and Judge in Revelation 19:11–16 and the final judgment in Revelation 20:11–15.

▶**Study Aim:** *To describe the visions of Christ as Victor and the final judgment*

STUDYING THE BIBLE

OUTLINE AND SUMMARY

 I. **Visions of Christ's Victory (Rev. 19:1–21)**

   1. Victory over the harlot (19:1–5)

   2. Announcement of the marriage of the Lamb (19:6–10)

   3. King of kings and Lord of lords (19:11–16)

   4. Victory over the beast and false prophet (19:17–21)

 II. **Final Victory (Revelation 20:1–15)**

   1. Binding Satan (20:1–3)

   2. The thousand-year reign (20:4–6)

   3. Final victory over Satan (20:7–10)

   4. Final judgment (20:11–15)

Heaven celebrated the destruction of the harlot (19:1–5). Many voices announced the marriage of the Lamb (19:6–10). A vision of Christ showed Him as Victor and Judge (19:11–16). The beast and false prophet shall be cast into a lake of fire (19:17–21). An angel shall bind Satan and throw him into a bottomless pit for a thousand years (20:1–3). Christ and His people shall reign for a thousand years (20:4–6). Satan shall be loosed and gather an army only to be thrown into the lake of fire (20:7–10). At the final judgment, those whose names are not in the book of life will experience the second death in the lake of fire (20:11–15).

I. Visions of Christ's Victory (Rev. 19:1–21)

1. Victory over the harlot (19:1–5)

Revelation 17–18 describe a great harlot (Babylon the great), her destruction, and the mourning over her fall. Revelation 19:1–3 is a vision of a great multitude in heaven praising God for His judgment on the great harlot. The twenty-four elders and four living beings join in these hallelujahs (vv. 4–5).

2. Announcement of the marriage of the Lamb (19:6–10)

John heard the voice of a great multitude announce that the time for the marriage of the Lamb had come (v. 6). The bride was ready (vv. 7–8).

A blessing was pronounced on those invited to the marriage of the Lamb (vv. 9–10).

3. King of kings and Lord of lords (19:11–16)

11 And I saw heaven opened, and behold a white horse; and he that sat upon him was called Faithful and True, and in righteousness he doth judge and make war.

John was allowed another glimpse into heaven. He saw a white horse and rider. The titles for the One on the white horse and the descriptions of what He does leave no doubt that the rider is Jesus Christ. Earlier Jesus had identified Himself as "the faithful and true witness" (Rev. 3:14; see also 1:5; 3:7). His faithfulness inspires faithfulness in His people. Because He is faithful, He will never allow His people to suffer alone. Because He is true, we know that truth will eventually prevail.

He is coming as a righteous Judge who will make war on Satan and all his evil allies. These two themes run throughout the rest of chapters 19—20. Christ is and will be the Judge; He is and will be the Victor.

12 His eyes were as a flame of fire, and on his head were many crowns; and he had a name written, that no man knew, but he himself.

Eyes like flames of fire was one of the descriptions of Christ in the initial vision of the Book of Revelation (1:14; see also 2:18). His eyes like fire are part of His role as Judge. His knowledge of each person is penetrating and piercing.

The dragon of Revelation 12:3, identified as Satan in 12:9, had seven heads and ten horns with a crown on each head. The beast from the sea in Revelation 13:1 had seven heads and ten horns with a crown on each horn. This shows that Satan and his ally had a certain amount of sovereignty. Christ, however, had "many crowns." His many crowns show that He has unlimited sovereignty, including authority over Satan and the sea beast.

In the ancient world, a person's name represented the person. Knowing a person's name gave someone power over the person whose name he knew (Gen. 32:29; Judg. 13:18). Thus God revealed some of His names, but only in such a way as to show that humans can never fathom all the mysteries of God (Exod. 3:14; 33:18–34:7). This may be the meaning of the last part of verse 12. Christ has revealed many of His names, but His full glory remains beyond our ability to fathom.

13 And he was clothed with a vesture dipped in blood: and his name is called The Word of God.

Bible students discuss whether the blood on His clothes represents His own blood (7:14), blood of the faithful martyrs (6:10), or blood from the flesh of His enemies (19:18). Since all three are images in the Book of Revelation, arguments can be made for each of these possibilities.

Christ is the eternal Word of God, who shares the very nature of God and through whom all things were created (John 1:1–3). "And the Word was made flesh, and dwelt among us, (and we beheld his glory, the glory as of the only begotten of the Father,) full of grace and truth" (John 1:14). This same Word of God will appear as Judge and Victor over evil.

14 And the armies which were in heaven followed him upon white horses, clothed in fine linen, white and clean.

Were these angels, or were they the redeemed people of God? Angels are described as heavenly hosts who serve God in various ways (Pss. 103:21; 148:2; Luke 2:13). Also, angels will be associated with the coming of Christ (Matt. 13:41; 16:27; 24:30–31). However, two factors favor the view that the armies in verse 14 describe the redeemed people of God. For one thing, the saints will share in Christ's sovereign reign (Rev. 2:26–27; 5:10; 20:4, 6). Revelation 17:14 tells how the King of kings and Lord of lords will overcome the beast and his forces; those with Christ are "called, and chosen, and faithful." Second, the description of clean, white clothes is used elsewhere for those whose robes have been washed white in the blood of the Lamb (7:14).

15 And out of his mouth goeth a sharp sword, that with it he should smite the nations: and he shall rule them with a rod of iron: and he treadeth the winepress of the fierceness and wrath of Almighty God.

16 And he hath on his vesture and on his thigh a name written, KING OF KINGS, AND LORD OF LORDS.

Christ is pictured entering battle armed with a sword that goes out of His mouth. This image is part of the initial vision of the Book of Revelation (1:16). Christ, the living Word of God, wins victory armed with the sword of His Word. Christ and His people do battle armed with the Word. The specific meaning in verse 15 is His word as Judge and King.

Psalm 2:9 provides the background for this and other references about the reign of Christ with a rod of iron (Rev. 2:27; 12:5). Part of His work in the last days will be as an instrument of divine wrath. He alone is qualified to perform such judgment, for He is King of kings and Lord of lords. None of the titles of Christ better describes His complete sovereignty and authority.

4. Victory over the beast and false prophet (19:17–21)

John heard an angel's voice calling all birds to come to the supper of God, and to feast on the flesh of armies and horses (vv. 17–18). John saw the beast of 13:1 and the kings of the earth gather for war against Christ (v. 19). The beast, false prophet (13:11–17), and those who worshiped them were seized and thrown into a lake of fire (v. 20). Their followers were slain and the birds devoured their flesh (v. 21).

II. Final Victory (Rev. 20:1–15)

1. Binding Satan (20:1–3)

John saw a mighty angel with the key to the bottomless pit and a huge chain (v. 1). The angel seized Satan, bound him for a thousand years, cast him into the pit, and set a seal on him (vv. 2–3).

2. The thousand-year reign (20:4–6)

John saw thrones of the faithful ones who reigned with Christ for a thousand years (v. 4). John heard a blessing pronounced on these who have part in the first resurrection because the second death has no power over them and because they shall reign as kings and priests with Christ.

The rest of the dead shall not live again until the end of the thousand years (vv. 5–6).

3. Final victory over Satan (20:7–10)

After the thousand years, Satan shall be loosed from his prison (v. 7). He shall deceive the nations, gather a great army, and surround the camp of the saints and the holy city. Then fire from God shall devour them (vv. 8–9). Finally, the devil shall be cast into the lake of fire, where the beast and false prophet are; and they shall be tormented forever (v. 10).

4. Final judgment (20:11–15)

11 And I saw a great white throne, and him that sat on it, from whose face the earth and the heaven fled away; and there was found no place for them.

When John saw a great white throne and someone seated on it, he also saw earth and heaven flee from His presence. Insofar as earth and heaven include evildoers, none will succeed in escaping (Rev. 6:16–17). The main idea here seems to be that the old earth and heaven vanish to make way for the new heaven and new earth (Rev. 21:1). Peter described this heaven passing away with a great noise and elements melting with fervent heat (2 Pet. 3:10).

12 And I saw the dead, small and great, stand before God; and the books were opened: and another book was opened, which is the book of life: and the dead were judged out of those things which were written in the books, according to their works.

13 And the sea gave up the dead which were in it; and death and hell delivered up the dead which were in them: and they were judged every man according to their works.

14 And death and hell were cast into the lake of fire. This is the second death.

15 And whosoever was not found written in the book of life was cast into the lake of fire.

Verse 13 describes the dead, regardless of earthly position, standing before God for judgment. The dead were summoned there, regardless of the place of their death. The sea, for example, gave up its dead. Death and hell gave up their dead. "Hell" is the Greek *hades*. It referred to the place of departed dead. Jesus used this word in describing the fate of the rich man in Luke 16:23.

The dead shall be judged from the book of life and from books showing their deeds. Since the book of life contains the names of the redeemed, anyone whose name is not in it stands condemned. The other books serve to verify their destiny based also on how they lived. Being cast into the lake of fire is referred to as the second death. This place of eternal punishment will already hold Satan, the beast, and the false prophet (19:20; 20:10).

This passage says nothing specifically about the judgment of those whose names are written in the book of life. This shows that the redeemed people of God will never be condemned and experience the second death. This does not mean that believers will not be judged and rewarded according to their works. Paul wrote that each of us must give account to God (Rom. 14:12). Paul included himself when he wrote, "We must all appear before the judgment seat of Christ; that every one may receive the things done in his body, according to that he hath done, whether it be good or bad" (2 Cor. 5:10; see also 1 Cor. 3:11–15).

Some Bible students think that the great white throne judgment will take place at a different time from the judgment of believers before the judgment seat of Christ. Others think they may be simultaneous. In either case, unbelievers will be condemned to hell because they are not in the book of life; and although Christians will be judged by their Lord, this will not mean condemnation to eternal punishment.

APPLYING THE BIBLE

1. Justice at the judgment. When General Robert E. Lee was the president of Washington College, in Lexington, Virginia, a student was brought before him who had broken the rules. In an attempt to calm the rattled nerves of the boy, the compassionate general said, "You need not be afraid; you will get justice here."

"I know, General," replied the boy. "That's what I'm scared of!"

In 19:1–5 John sees the "great whore," which had shed the blood of the saints, being judged by God. The "great whore" was Rome (see ch. 17), and she was brought down to ruins. As we know from history, this, indeed, took place. God's judgment is always just.

2. The marriage supper. The Old Testament writer employed the metaphor of marriage to indicate the bond of love between God and Israel. But Jesus also used it to describe His love for all believers. This is how it is used here (19:7–10).

A wedding is a wonderful thing: the beautiful bride (vv. 7–8); the handsome groom (vv. 7, 9); and all the festivities that accompany a wedding (v. 9).

John writes to the persecuted saints in Asia Minor and encourages them to be faithful to Jesus for the day would soon come when they would be forever united with their Lord (vv. 7–10).

3. Eyes only for Jesus. There is an ancient legend that tells about a beautiful Christian girl who was condemned to death in a Roman arena where she would be torn to pieces for the amusement of her pagan persecutors. Among the spectators was a Roman prince who dearly loved the girl and pled for her release but to no avail. When the lion's cage was opened, much to the surprise of the spectators, the fierce lions didn't attack her. She appeared to be at perfect peace. Her persecutors declared that she "was charmed by the gods" and released her. When she was led out of the arena and reunited with her lover, he asked her the secret of her composure and she replied, "I had eyes only for you."

The saints in Asia Minor had suffered much for their faith, but John writes to encourage them to be faithful to Jesus and have eyes only for Him (vv. 11–16). The day was coming when suffering would be over, and they would meet their Lord, the King of kings and the Lord of lords, face to face (v. 16). It would be worth it all when they saw Jesus.

4. Doctor Faustus's bargain with Satan. In his play *The Tragical History of Doctor Faustus*, English author Christopher Marlowe tells how the legendary Faustus struck a bargain with the devil. In the bargain, the devil would be the servant of Faustus for twenty-four years. The devil would give Faustus everything he wanted, but at the end of the twenty-four years the devil would claim the soul of Faustus. At the end, Faustus sees what a terrible bargain he has made when Satan says to him:

O Faustus,
Now hast thou but one bare hour to live
and then, thou must be damned perpetually.

Satan is powerful, but his power is limited by Christ. In 12:2 Satan has seven crowns upon his seven heads. In 13:1, Satan has ten crowns on his ten heads. He is powerful. But in 19:12, Jesus has "many crowns" on his head. The message for the saints in the first century, and for us today, is that Christ is more powerful than Satan and Christ will have the last word when Satan is cast into hell. The saints must be faithful to Christ even when they were being persecuted for His sake.

5. The hopelessness of hell. Over the huge doors of the prison de la Roquette, in Paris, are inscribed the words, "Abandon hope, all ye who enter here!" The prison, set apart for criminals who are condemned to die for their crimes, offers absolutely no hope.

Those who live without Jesus as their Savior have no hope for eternity (Eph. 2:12). Their hopeless condition is clearly seen in 20:15.

TEACHING THE BIBLE

▶ *Main Idea:* Jesus will ultimately be victorious over evil and be crowned King of kings and Lord of lords.

▶ *Suggested Teaching Aim:* To lead adults to crown Jesus as King of kings and Lord of lords.

A TEACHING OUTLINE

1. Use a writing activity to introduce the Bible study.

2. Use a chart to identify the names of Jesus in these passages.

3. Use questions-answers to search for biblical truth.

4. Use questions to make the Bible study personal.

5. Use "How to Become a Christian" feature to acquaint members with how to commit their lives to Christ.

Introduce the Bible Study

As members enter, ask them to go to a chalkboard or a large sheet of paper and write the most unusual name of a person they have ever heard. Read aloud some of the names and ask: What's in a name? Why are names important? Why do couples normally spend so much time picking the right name? Point out that our Scripture passage today mentions several names of Jesus; it also mentions that Jesus has one name that no human knows.

Search for Biblical Truth

Ask members to open their Bibles to Revelation 19:11–16 and skim those verse to identify all the names and titles of Jesus. Write these on a chalkboard or a large sheet of paper. (Faithful, True, Word of God, King of kings, Lord of lords.) After members have listed the names, use "Studying the Bible" and the following questions to explain each of the names: What effect does Jesus' faithfulness have on His people (v. 11)? As a righteous judge, on whom will Jesus make war (v. 11—Satan and his allies)? What description of Jesus from 1:14 is used in verse 12? What was significant about Jesus' "many crowns" (v. 12a)? What was significant about humans not knowing a name of Jesus (v. 12b)? Whose blood had Jesus' clothes been dipped in (v. 13)? Why is Jesus referred to as the "Word of God" in this passage (v. 13)? Who makes up the army (v. 14)? What description of Jesus from 1:16 is used in verse 15? How does the description of Jesus with a sharp sword coming out of His mouth relate to the title, "Word of God"? What does the title "Lord of lords and King of kings" mean to you?

Use "Studying the Bible" to summarize briefly 20:1–10. Ask members to look at 20:11–15. Use "Studying the Bible" and the following questions: Who was seated on the great white throne (v. 11)? What purpose did earth and heaven's fleeing serve (v. 11)? What is the purpose of the book of life (v. 12)? What happens to those whose names are not found in the book (v. 15)? What assurance does this give believers?

DISCUSS: Which name of Jesus means the most to you? Why? Which one comforts the most? Why? Which one is the most fearful? Why?

Give the Truth a Personal Focus

Ask: How do you feel about Christ's final victory and judgment? Are you ready for it? (If you have members in your class who are not Christians, pray that the Holy Spirit will use this class as an opportunity to lead them to Christ.

Close with a prayer that all members will have their names written in the Lamb's book of life.

A New Heaven and Earth

Basic Passage: Revelation 21:1–22:5

Focal Passages: Revelation 21:1–7, 22–27

The final chapters in Revelation describe the completion of God's redemptive work and the blessed state of His people. God seeks to communicate the glory of heaven by describing what will be there and by naming things that will not be there.

▶**Study Aim:** *To describe the new heaven and new earth in terms of what will be there and what will not be there*

STUDYING THE BIBLE

OUTLINE AND SUMMARY

   I. **New Creation (Rev. 21:1–8)**

      1. Introduction (21:1–4)

      2. Completion of salvation (21:5–6)

      3. Challenge (21:7–8)

  II. **New City (Rev. 21:9—22:5)**

      1. Description of the city (21:9–21)

      2. God's glory (21:22–27)

      3. Paradise restored (22:1–5)

The new heaven and new earth will have a holy city in which God dwells with His people and takes away all that blights earthly life (21:1–4). God who began all things will bring His purposes to a consummation (21:5–6). Those who overcome will inherit all things, but those who reject God will be in the lake of fire (22:7–8). The holy city will be of gold and precious stones (21:9–21). The new earth will have no temple and no sun because of God's glorious presence (21:22–27). The holy city will have a river of water of life and a tree of life (22:1–5).

I. New Creation (Rev. 21:1–8)

1. Introduction (21:1–4)

1 And I saw a new heaven and a new earth: for the first heaven and the first earth were passed away; and there was no more sea.

John had seen earth and heaven flee away before the face of the One on the great white throne (Rev. 20:11). Beginning in Revelation 21:1, John saw a new heaven and a new earth. The words "no more sea" reflect the fears of the ancient world of the sea. Seas were wild stormy places of danger and death for many who ventured out on the seas. John also reflected his own circumstances as an exile on a small island, separated from fellow Christians by the sea.

2 And I John saw the holy city, new Jerusalem, coming down from God out of heaven, prepared as a bride adorned for her husband.

A central feature of the new heaven and new earth will be a holy city. It will be a new Jerusalem, in contrast to the earthly Jerusalem, which had desecrated its intended purpose by killing God's messengers and even God's Son (see Matt. 23:37). Notice that it is pictured as coming down from God out of heaven. It will be no earthly utopia erected by human initiative and efforts. This holy city will be a gift and creation of God.

The holy city will be adorned as a bride for her husband. Paul wrote of the church as the bride of Christ (Eph. 5:25–33). Revelation 19:7–9 describes an announcement of the marriage supper of the Lamb. In Revelation 21:2, John saw the bride come to be joined with the Lamb. Notice that the holy city describes both the people of God and their eternal abode. This double meaning was used in Revelation 17–18 to describe the antithesis of the new Jerusalem and the bride of Christ: the great harlot was described as an evil city, Babylon the great.

> **3 And I heard a great voice out of heaven saying, Behold, the tabernacle of God is with men, and he will dwell with them, and they shall be his people, and God himself shall be with them, and be their God.**

Verse 3 describes the central feature of the new heaven and new earth: perfect fellowship with God. The word "tabernacle" reminds us of the tabernacle where God's presence rested among His people, but no one could see His face and live (Exod. 33:20). Only a few were allowed to approach Him and carry back His messages. When the living Word became flesh and dwelt among people, God was with those who recognized Christ as Immanuel, God with us (John 1:14; Matt. 1:23). Believers know God through faith in His Son, but believers throughout the ages have dreamed of a time when they would see and know God face to face (Matt. 5:8). John heard a great voice announcing that God's tabernacle or dwelling place would now be among His redeemed people.

> **4 And God shall wipe away all tears from their eyes; and there shall be no more death, neither sorrow, nor crying, neither shall there be any more pain: for the former things are passed away.**

This is one of the most precious promises of the Bible. The Word of God seeks to communicate the glories of heaven by telling us some of the things that will not be there. Because God will be there, all that blights earthly existence will not be there. God Himself will be the Comforter who wipes away all tears from our eyes. Death, that dogged reminder of our sinful heritage, will have been conquered and cast into the lake of fire (1 Cor. 15:26; Rev. 20:14). Sorrow and crying will be no more because the causes of grief and tears—death and pain—will be no more. They are dreadful realities in this earthly existence; but when this earth and its order shall pass away, they will pass away with it.

If you were God and you wanted to communicate to earthbound minds what heaven will be like, how would you do it? One way that God did it was to remind us of some of the things that make earthly life a vale of tears. Then with a shout of victory we are told that none of these things will be in God's new creation. I don't believe God intended to limit the list just to what was named in verse 4. I believe that the message of verse 4 is that none of what blights earthly life will be in heaven. We can get some idea of the glory of heaven by considering it in this way: everything that makes earthly life painful and deadly will be no more; everything that makes earthly life joyful and fruitful will be magnified by the direct presence of God.

2. Completion of salvation (21:5–6)

5 And he that sat upon the throne said, Behold, I make all things new. And he said unto me, Write: for these words are true and faithful.

6 And he said unto me, It is done. I am Alpha [AL fuh] and Omega [oh MEG uh], the beginning and the end. I will give unto him that is athirst of the fountain of the water of life freely.

Paul wrote of each person in Christ as a new creation, in which "old things are passed away; behold, all things are become new" (2 Cor. 5:17). God used similar language to describe the new heaven and new earth. He commanded John to write because these words bear the stamp of divine truth and trustworthiness.

"It is done" means literally "they have come to pass." Jesus' words from the cross, "it is finished," signaled the victorious completion of His atoning work (John 19:30). God's words "it is done" declare the completion of God's redemptive purposes. All the redeemed will have been gathered home; and sin, death, and Satan will have been totally and forever vanquished.

As in Revelation 1:8, God spoke of Himself as Alpha and Omega, the first and last letters of the Greek alphabet. He is the beginning and the ending because He is the eternal Creator who created this universe and who will create for His children a new heaven and a new earth. God promised that in that new creation, all who are thirsty will drink of the fountain of living water freely (see Isa. 55:1; John 4:14; Rev. 22:17).

3. Challenge (21:7–8)

7 He that overcometh shall inherit all things; and I will be his God, and he shall be my son.

As we have seen, the challenge to overcome (literally, to gain the victory) is found over and over in Revelation (2:7, 11, 26; 3:5, 12, 21). These challenges to win the victory are accompanied by God's promises to those who overcome. God promised to be their God and to count them as children in the family of the new creation. As such they would receive their full inheritance from their Heavenly Father.

Verse 8 looks back to the scenes of judgment in Revelation 20:11–15 and reminds us that not all people are God's children. Verse 8 lists those groups that were not in the new creation.

II. New City (Rev. 21:9–22:5)

1. Description of the city (21:9–21)

An angel called John for a closer look at the bride of Christ (21:9). The Spirit took him up into a high mountain for a view of the holy Jerusalem (21:10). John saw the glory of God like precious stones (21:11). He saw the wall and gates with each gate named for a tribe of Israel (21:12–13). He saw the foundations named for the twelve apostles (21:14). The angel with a measuring rod described the dimensions of the city and its wall (21:15–17). The wall was of jasper and the city was pure gold (21:18). The foundations were garnished with precious stones, each gate was a pearl, and the streets were gold (21:19–21).

2. God's glory (21:22–27)

22 And I saw no temple therein: for the Lord God Almighty and the Lamb are the temple of it.

23 And the city had no need of the sun, neither of the moon, to shine in it: for the glory of God did lighten it, and the Lamb is the light thereof.

The temple was the center of old Jerusalem. Like the tabernacle before it, the temple represented the presence of God among the people. His glorious presence was promised as long as His people served Him. But it was a mediated presence and veiled glory, and the people so sinned that His glory left the temple (Ezek. 10:18; 11:23). The new Jerusalem will have no need for a temple, because God and the Lamb will dwell directly with the redeemed. The old earth is lighted and warmed by the sun, with the moon providing some light even at night. Since God Himself and the Lamb will be the light for the new creation, there will be no sun or moon.

24 And the nations of them which are saved shall walk in the light of it: and the kings of the earth do bring their glory and honour into it.

25 And the gates of it shall not be shut at all by day: for there shall be no night there.

26 And they shall bring the glory and honour of the nations into it.

27 And there shall in no wise enter into it any thing that defileth, neither whatsoever worketh abomination, or maketh a lie: but they which are written in the Lamb's book of life.

Previously in Revelation, "nations" and "kings" stood for people and leaders who gave their allegiance to Satan and his allies (11:18; 18:3, 23). Such nations and kings were defeated and made subject to Christ (19:15). The nations and kings of Revelation 21:24 describe people of the new earth who are redeemed people of God. We know little about how life will be organized in the new earth, but we know that all honor and glory will be given to God.

Gates were necessary in ancient cities. Since night was a time of danger from enemy attacks, gates were closed. The new Jerusalem will have a wall and gates, but the gates will never be closed because there will be neither enemies nor night. The open gates are a sign of total security and safety.

Verse 27, like verse 8, reminds us that nothing or no one who is evil will enter the city. Such people and things have no part in the new earth or the holy city. Only those whose names are written in the Lamb's book of life will abide there.

3. Paradise restored (22:1–5)

John saw a river of water of life proceeding out of the throne of God and of the Lamb (22:1). He saw a tree of life with leaves for the healing of the nations (22:2). The curse of sin will be no more because God's servants shall see His face and have His name on their foreheads (22:3–4). There will be no night, no candles, and no sun, for God will lighten them and reign forever (22:5).

APPLYING THE BIBLE

1. No fear in heaven. In January 1960, a smelly wretch named Grisha Sikalenko appeared before his neighbors in Tsirkuny in the Ukraine. His neighbors were shocked because they thought he had died a hero's death fighting the Germans. The truth was that on the night his company marched off to war, Grisha deserted and sneaked home. His mother made for him a hiding place under the manure pile at the back of the goat shed, and for eighteen years he existed in a living grave. In the winter he almost froze to death, and in the summer he nearly suffocated. But his fear of being found and prosecuted made him stay in his miserable hovel. When he finally emerged, he found that his fears were groundless for the statute of limitations had long since made him immune from prosecution.

The Jews were not sea-going people. When John says there is "no more sea" (v. 1) in heaven, he is telling his readers that our greatest fears on earth will be barred from heaven!

2. Heaven, pure and holy. When one walks down the streets of our largest cities, one observes how dirty and filthy they are. But the alleyways are even grimmer, filled with huge piles of garbage. Humankind dirties and ruins everything we touch. Even nature suffers, because of human sins. But John saw a new Jerusalem, coming down from God out of heaven, prepared as a bride adorned for her husband (v. 2). Nothing is purer or more beautiful than an innocent bride coming down the aisle to be united in marriage with her groom. This is a graphic picture of heaven's purity.

3. No disappointments in heaven. Over the great doorway of the cathedral at Milan, Italy, three inscriptions have been carved. On the first arch appear the words, "All that which pleases is but for a moment." Over the second arch are sculpted the words, "All that troubles is but for a moment." And on the great central arch are the words, "That only which is eternal is important."

The most important thing in life is to be sure we are going to heaven when we die. John says there are no disappointments or separations there (v. 4).

4. Does God know you are coming? A small boy visiting New York City was riding up the elevator of the Empire State Building. As they traveled higher and higher, the little fellow looked down, gulped, and asked his father, "Daddy, does God know we are coming?"

It's a good question. But more important is the question, "Do *you* know you are going to heaven when you die?" You can know. Fully trust in Christ's shed blood and you *will* know (John 14:6).

TEACHING THE BIBLE

‣ *Main Idea:* Heaven is a place for God and His people.

‣ *Suggested Teaching Aim:* To lead adults to describe who will be in heaven.

Introduce the Bible Study

IN ADVANCE, arrange for enough hymnals for each member to have one. As members enter, ask them to find three of their favorite hymns about heaven. On a chalkboard or a large sheet of paper, list these hymns and rank them to find the three favorite hymns about heaven. Save this list to use at the conclusion of the lesson.

Search for Biblical Truth

NOTE: If you choose not to form two groups, you can do this as a class. Ask half the class to read Revelation 21:1–7 and the other half to read 21:22–27. Give the half of the class assigned 21:1–7 a copy of the following questions without answers and ask them to answer them. Allow six to eight minutes for study and then call for reports.

Group 1—The New Creation
Revelation 21:1–7

1. What was the most obvious absence in the new heaven and new earth (v. 1)? (No sea.)
2. Why do you think this was so? (Sea was fearful to nomads.)
3. What do you think is the significance of the New Jerusalem's coming down out of heaven? (No earthly utopia.)
4. What is the central feature of the new heaven and the new earth (v. 3)? (Fellowship with God; would see Him face to face.)
5. What act of tenderness will God perform (v. 4)? (Wipe away tears.)
6. Why will there not be any more sorrow and crying (v. 4)? (Death and pain—the causes of sorrow—will not be in heaven.)
7. What does the promise in verse 5 mean to you?
8. Verse 5 is the third time the phrase "Alpha and Omega" appears in Revelation (after 1:8, 11) and it will appear in 22:13. In 21:6 the reference is to God; in the other cases, it refers to Jesus. What can you draw from this? (They are one.)
9. What will God give His children (v. 6)? (Water of life.)
10. What benefit do we receive if we overcome? (God will be our God and we will be His children.)

Group 2—The New City
Revelation 21:22–27

1. What building will not be in the New Jerusalem (v. 22)? (Temple.)
2. Why will there be no temple in heaven (v. 22)? (Temple represented God on earth; He will dwell with us in heaven.)
3. Why will night not exist in heaven (v. 25)? (There is no sun or moon—v. 23.)
4. What will the nations of the earth give God (v. 24)? (Glory and honor.)

5. Why are the gates never closed in heaven (v. 25)? (Nothing evil to keep out.)
6. Who/what will not be in heaven (v. 27a)? (Anything or anyone who is evil.)
7. Who will be in heaven (v. 27b)? (Those whose names are written in the Lamb's book of life.)
8. What must we do to be certain our names are written in the Lamb's book of life?

DISCUSS: Which feature of heaven gives you the most comfort?

Give the Truth a Personal Focus

Refer to the list of favorite hymns. Ask: What about the hymns you chose makes them your favorites? Is it the words? music? where you learned them? Sing or read the words of the hymn that was ranked first. Close in a prayer that all members will know beyond any shadow of a doubt that they will experience heaven.